Physical Geography
A Laboratory Manual

Third Edition

John J. Hidore
University of North Carolina
Greensboro, North Carolina

Michael C. Roberts
Simon Fraser University
Burnaby, British Columbia

Burgess Publishing Company
Minneapolis, Minnesota

Copyright © 1985, 1978, 1974 by John J. Hidore and Michael C. Roberts
Printed in the United States of America
ISBN: 0-8087-4763-0

J I H G F E D C

Contents

Preface

This laboratory manual is designed to be used in an introductory course in physical geography where laboratory work is an integral part of the course. It can be used along with, and as a supplement to, any basic textbook in physical geography. The exercises are designed to acquaint the student with the kinds of materials and data with which the physical geographer works, such as topographic maps, aerial photographs, weather maps, and numerical information. There is also an introduction to some of the methods for analyzing numerical data.

One of the problems in incorporating a laboratory into an introductory physical geography course, as with any other teaching laboratory, is the assembling of the equipment and materials needed. This manual is intended to reduce the extent of this problem by including a series of weather maps, topographic maps, matched pairs of aerial photographs suitable for stereoscopic viewing, and field data pertaining to the environment. Some of the exercises are traditional in the topics covered, and others are directed at current environmental problems.

For many students enrolling in a college-level physical geography course, it will be their last formal academic exposure to the topic. Throughout their lives, however, exposure to physical geography will continue, and the exercises contained here are designed to give the students a greater awareness and understanding of the environment in which they live. For those students continuing in the field, the exercises should serve as an introduction to methodology and some current problems.

The third edition differs from the previous edition in several ways: (1) many of the exercises have been rewritten to make them clearer, (2) new material has been added to update some of the exercises, and (3) some entirely new exercises have been added and some exercises from previous editions have been deleted.

Some of the changes from the second edition are these: a map on the distribution of ash fall from Mount Saint Helens during the major eruption of 1980 has been added to Exercise 1; two exercises on wind systems from previous editions have been combined into Exercise 9; Exercise 12 on climatic classification has been substantially rewritten for clarification and new data have been added; and Exercise 13 includes a new weather map.

Among the new exercises are the following: Exercise 7 focuses on the seasons from the perspective of the water balance. Included are data related to the shifting of the rainfall zone north and south in Africa with the seasons. Other data on precipitation and runoff stress seasonality in North America. Exercise 8 is on the probability and intensity of precipitation. Daily precipitation data for a year are included for one station so students can determine frequencies as well as intervals between episodes and length of precipitation episodes. Exercise 10 is on the water balance. Data for potential evaporation, precipitation, and actual evaporation are provided for a number of stations. The students can calculate moisture surplus or deficiencies. Precipitation and runoff data are provided for a watershed so that the seasonal water balance can be determined. Exercise 33, "A Case Study of an Environmental Hazard—Land Subsidence in Long Beach, California," contains maps and tables of data related to land subsidence resulting from the withdrawal of oil. Exercise 34, "The Tides," contains daily data for three months for Boston, Massachusetts, as well as data on the range of tides from New York City to the Bay of Fundy. At the end of the manual there are new sections dealing with soil classification, metric conversion tables, and most importantly, a selection of air photographs that can be removed from the manual for use with mirror stereoscopes.

We invite users of this manual to forward suggestions on the content of the manual and to notify us of any errors that are detected.

Name: _____

Laboratory section: _____

Radiation and Temperature

Solar radiation is the primary source of energy in the earth environment, although the earth intercepts but a very small portion of the total radiation emitted by the sun. While the amount of radiation reaching the earth is fairly constant throughout the year, the amount of radiation reaching any point on the ground varies greatly through time. A variety of factors affect the spatial variation in radiant energy reaching the surface. Among the more important is the intensity of solar radiation at the surface. Intensity is affected by the amount of radiation reflected and scattered back to space, the amount of energy absorbed directly by the atmosphere, and the angle of the solar beam with the surface. This difference in intensity of solar radiation is the primary variable in the latitudinal distribution of temperature.

To illustrate the effects of angle of the solar beam on radiation intensity, Figure 3.1A shows the beam of one square unit perpendicular to the surface. It illuminates an area on

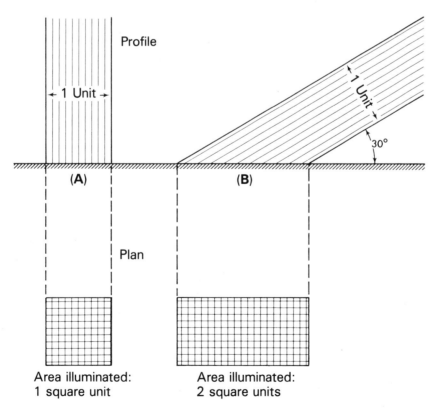

Figure 3.1. Effect of the angle of radiation on intensity

the surface of one square unit. When the angle is reduced to 30 degrees, as in Figure 3.1B, a solar beam of one square unit illuminates a larger area—in this particular case, an area twice as large. Since the same amount of energy is being spread over a larger area, the intensity (energy per area) must be less. Since the area is twice as great in Figure 3.1B, the intensity must be just one half as great as in Figure 3.1A. Table 3.1 gives the intensity of the solar beam for various angles as a percentage of a perpendicular beam. Note that for an angle of 30 degrees, the radiation intensity is 50% of that of a perpendicular beam, which is in agreement with the illustration in Figure 3.1. The intensity of solar radiation varies as the sine of the angle of the sun above the horizon, and Table 3.1 is, in fact, a table of sines.

PROBLEMS

1. Figure 3.2 is a simplified diagram of the cross section of the atmosphere. Measure the length of solar beam A and solar beam B. The ratio of the length of travel through the atmosphere of beam B to A is _____:1. This greater length of travel increases the amount of reflection, absorption, and scattering of radiation back to space, making the actual radiation received at the surface even less than that due to solar angle alone.

Table 3.1. Intensity of Solar Radiation[a]

Angle of Beam	Degrees - units									
	0°	1°	2°	3°	4°	5°	6°	7°	8°	9°
0°	00.00	01.75	03.49	05.23	06.98	08.72	10.45	12.19	13.92	15.64
10°	17.36	19.08	20.79	22.50	24.19	25.88	27.56	29.24	30.90	32.56
20°	34.20	35.84	37.46	39.07	40.67	42.26	43.84	45.40	46.95	48.48
30°	50.00	51.50	52.99	54.46	55.92	57.36	58.78	60.18	61.57	62.93
40°	64.28	65.61	66.91	68.20	69.47	70.71	71.93	73.14	74.31	75.47
50°	76.60	77.71	78.80	79.86	80.90	81.92	82.90	83.87	84.80	85.72
60°	86.60	87.46	88.29	89.10	89.88	90.63	91.36	92.05	92.72	93.36
70°	93.97	94.55	95.11	95.63	96.13	96.59	97.03	97.44	97.81	98.16
80°	98.48	98.77	99.03	99.25	99.45	99.62	99.76	99.86	99.94	99.98

[a]Radiation intensity for given angles of solar inclination expressed as a percent of the radiation intensity of a beam perpendicular to the surface. To locate the relative intensity for 53 degrees, read down the left column to 50 and then across the row to 3. The relative intensity for 53 degrees of solar inclination is 79.86.

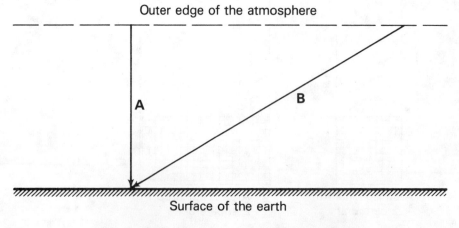

Outer edge of the atmosphere

A   B

Surface of the earth

Figure 3.2. Cross section of atmosphere

In Figure 3.3 draw a line through points B_1 and B_2 and label it the circle of illumination. Extend line $C_1 C_2$ through the circle and label it the solar equator. Next construct a line from the center of the circle through D_1, a line tangent to the circle at D_1, and a line representing a ray of solar energy from D_2 to D_1.

At any one time half the earth is illuminated by solar radiation. The intensity of the radiation decreases as the distance from C_1 increases. The intensity of the radiation decreases as a result of the progressively lower angle of the beam and the greater distance the radiation has to travel through the atmosphere. The angle of the radiation with the surface at point D is 30 degrees, the same as in the example in Figure 3.2. Hence, the solar radiation is less than half what it is at point C_1. The maximum intensity of the radiation is at C_1, which is the solar equator.

2. For each of the cities in Table 3.2 determine the altitude of the sun, the relative intensity of solar radiation, and the length of the day at the time of the equinox (use Table 3.1). Figure 3.3 and Table 3.2, which you have just completed, illustrate the earth-sun relationship at the time of the equinox.

Table 3.2. Effect of Latitude on Radiation Intensity

Location	Latitude	Altitude of the Sun (°)	Radiation Intensity (%)
Nome, Alas.	65°N	————	————
Edmonton, Alberta	55°N	————	————
Portland, Oregon	45°N	————	————
Oklahoma City, Oklahoma	35°N	————	————
São Paulo, Brazil	23½°S	————	————
Punta Arenas, Chile	53°S	————	————

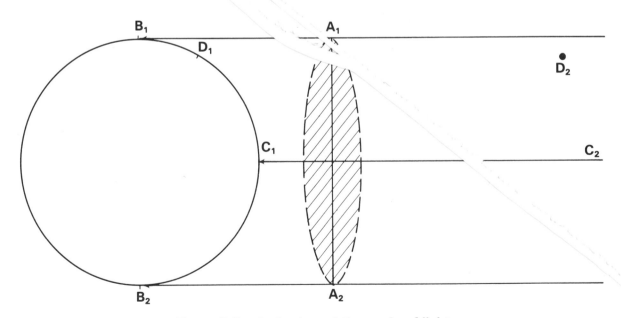

Figure 3.3. Latitude and the angle of light

EXERCISE **4**

The Seasons—I

The seasons of the year, which are such important regulators of life, are associated with temperature and moisture changes throughout the year. Seasonal changes in temperature result primarily from the inclination of the earth on its axis and the revolution of the earth about the sun. These two phenomena produce changes in the intensity and duration of sunlight at most points on the earth's surface.

While the curvature of the earth is partially responsible for the varying intensity of radiation, the problem is compounded as a result of the changing position of the heat equator. As the earth revolves about the sun with its axis of rotation inclined 66½ degrees with the plane of the ecliptic, the perpendicular rays of the sun shift latitudinally over an angular distance of 47 degrees. This shifting of the perpendicular beam produces large imbalances of heating between the northern and southern hemispheres.

PROBLEMS

1. In Figure 4.1, draw in parallels at 23½ degrees north and south and at 66½ degrees north and south. Draw in the circle of illumination. Label the Tropic of Cancer, Tropic of Capricorn, Arctic Circle, and Antarctic Circle. Next, draw in several lines representing beams of solar radiation. Place two of these at right angles to the circle

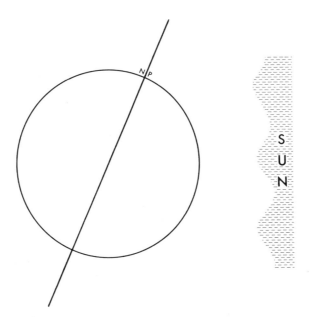

Figure 4.1. Earth at summer solstice

of illumination and tangent to the surface. Place a third beam perpendicular to the earth's surface at the Tropic of Cancer. This diagram represents the radiation conditions as they exist at the time of the summer solstice.

Repeat the process for Figure 4.2, which, when completed, represents the radiation conditions for the winter solstice. Now complete Table 4.1.

2. Between latitudes _____ degrees north and _____ degrees south, the sun is directly overhead twice each year. The latitudinal zone in which the noon sun is observed always to be south of the zenith is _____ degrees north to _____ degrees north, and the zone in which the noon sun is always observed north of the zenith is _____ degrees south to _____ degrees south. The maximum variation in the angle of the noon sun experienced at any point on the earth's surface is 47 degrees. The latitudinal zone which experiences this variation extends from _____ degrees to _____ degrees on either side of the equator. In both the equatorial zone (0 degrees–23½ degrees) and the polar zone (66½ degrees–90 degrees) the variation in the angle of the noon sun is less than 47 degrees through the year.

3. Based upon the angle of solar radiation, determine whether Minneapolis (45 degrees north) has more or less intense radiation than the equator on the following dates:

   a. Spring equinox (March 21)   _____
   b. Summer solstice (June 22)   _____
   c. Fall equinox (September 23)   _____
   d. Winter solstice (December 22) _____

Figure 4.2.   Earth at winter solstice

Table 4.1.   Angle of Radiation by Season

	March 21	June 22	September 23	December 22
Latitude of vertical rays of the sun	_____	_____	_____	_____
Tangent rays of the sun in the northern hemisphere	_____	_____	_____	_____
Tangent rays of the sun in the southern hemisphere	_____	_____	_____	_____
Name associated with each date	_____	_____	_____	_____

4. St. Louis, Missouri, is located at a latitude of approximately 39 degrees north. Using the data provided in Table 4.2, determine the date in the spring when the radiation intensity at St. Louis becomes equal to the intensity at the equator: _____. For a period of time after this date, the radiation intensity in St. Louis (barring the effects of atmospheric pollution) will be greater than at the equator. As the perpendicular beam of solar radiation moves southward again after the summer solstice, there will again occur a time when solar radiation at St. Louis is nearly the same as at the equator. That date is _____ . There is thus a period of about _____ weeks when solar intensity in the latitude of St. Louis is greater than it is at the equator. The same relationship can be determined for all locations in the United States with latitudes south of 47 degrees north.

5. Latitudinal changes in insolation are also affected by the varying length of the day. At the time of the equinoxes, the length of the day is equal everywhere, 12 hr of daylight and 12 hr of darkness. During the rest of the year, there are inequities between the northern hemisphere and the southern hemisphere. Table 4.3 shows the lengths of the daylight period for the summer and winter solstices, the longest and shortest days of the year respectively. At the time of the summer solstice, determine the length of the daylight period for the equator and for Minneapolis.

a. Equator _____
b. Minneapolis _____

Table 4.2. Declination of the Sun on Selected Days of the Year

Day	January	February	March	April	May	June
1	− 23°04′	− 17°19′	− 7°53′	+ 4°14′	+ 14°50′	+ 21°57′
5	22 42	16 10	6 21	5 46	16 02	22 38
9	22 13	14 55	4 48	7 17	17 09	22 52
13	21 37	13 37	3 14	8 46	18 11	23 10
17	20 54	12 15	1 39	10 12	19 09	23 22
21	20 05	10 50	− 0 05	11 35	20 02	23 27
25	19 09	9 23	+ 1 30	12 56	20 49	23 25
29	18 08	-	3 04	14 13	21 30	23 17

Day	July	August	September	October	November	December
1	+ 23°10′	+ 18°14′	+ 8°35′	− 2°53′	− 14°11′	− 21°40′
5	22 52	17 12	7 07	4 26	15 27	22 16
9	22 28	16 06	5 37	5 58	16 38	22 45
13	21 57	14 55	4 06	7 29	17 45	23 06
17	21 21	13 41	2 34	8 58	18 48	23 20
21	20 38	12 23	+ 1 01	10 25	19 45	23 26
25	19 50	11 02	− 0 32	11 50	20 36	23 25
29	18 57	9 39	2 06	13 12	21 21	23 17

From U.S. Naval Observatory, 1950, *The American ephemeris and nautical almanac for the year 1950*, table by R. J. List (Washington, D. C.).

Table 4.3.   Length of Daylight for Intervals of 1 Degree of Latitude[a]

	0°	1°	2°	3°	4°	5°	6°	7°	8°	9°
0°	12:07 12:07	12:11 12:04	12:15 12:00	12:18 11:57	12:22 11:53	12:25 11:50	12:29 11:46	12:32 11:43	12:36 11:39	12:39 11:36
10°	12:43 11:33	12:47 11:29	12:50 11:25	12:54 11:21	12:58 11:18	13:02 11:14	13:05 11:10	13:09 11:07	13:13 11:03	13:17 10:59
20°	13:21 10:55	13:25 10:51	13:29 10:47	13:33 10:43	13:37 10:39	13:42 10:35	13:47 10:30	13:51 10:26	13:56 10:22	14:00 10:17
30°	14:05 10:12	14:10 10:08	14:15 10:03	14:20 9:58	14:26 9:53	14:31 9:48	14:37 9:42	14:43 9:37	14:49 9:31	14:55 9:25
40°	15:02 9:19	15:08 9:13	15:15 9:07	15:22 9:00	15:30 8:53	15:38 8:46	15:46 8:38	15:54 8:30	16:03 8:22	16:13 8:14
50°	16:23 8:04	16:33 7:54	16:45 7:44	16:57 7:33	17:09 7:22	17:23 7:10	17:38 6:57	17:54 6:42	18:11 6:27	18:31 6:10
60°	18:53 5:52	19:17 5:32	19:45 5:09	20:19 4:42	21:02 4:18	22:03 3:34	- 2:46	- 1:30	- -	- -

[a]The upper figure in each pair of figures represents the longest day, and the lower figure represents the shortest day. To find the length of daylight for 37 degrees, read down to 30 degrees in the left column and across the row to 7 degrees. The longest day at 37 degrees is 14 hr, 43 min. Note that the two periods do not add up to 24 hr because daylight is measured when the rim of the sun, rather than the center of the sun, is visible.

In late June and early July, most of the United States not only receives more intense radiation but receives it for a longer period of time each day than do places at the equator. In terms of radiant energy received at the earth's surface, the United States in the summertime receives as much as or more radiation than is being received at the equator. It would logically follow that if areas north of the Tropic of Cancer receive more radiation than the areas near the equator, temperatures recorded in the midlatitudes would be greater than those at the equator. This is the case. The highest temperature recorded in the northern hemisphere is 57.7 °C (136 °F) at El Azizia, Libya, on 13 September 1922 at latitude 33 degrees north; the highest recorded in North America is 56.6 °C (134 °F) on 10 July 1913 in Death Valley, California, at latitude 36 degrees north. So, contrary to popular belief, the highest temperatures occur in midlatitudes rather than near the equator.

EXERCISE 5

Atmospheric Humidity

Atmospheric humidity is the result of the presence of water vapor in the atmosphere. Water in the gaseous state is one of the many gases that make up a given unit volume of air. The amount of water vapor that the air contains varies greatly.

Since all gases exert pressure, the water vapor in the air contributes part of the total atmospheric pressure. The unit for measuring pressure is the millibar (mb), which is equal to a force of 1000 dynes per cm² (a dyne is the force needed to accelerate a mass of 1 g by 1 cm/sec).

SATURATED VAPOR PRESSURE

The maximum amount of water the air can hold (saturated vapor pressure) is associated with the temperature of the air. The saturated vapor pressure for temperatures from − 59 °C to + 49 °C is given in Table 5.1.

PROBLEMS

1. List the saturated vapor pressure for each pair of temperatures listed below and determine the differences in vapor pressure.

   − 12 °C (10 °F) _____   10 °C (50 °F) _____   32 °C (90 °F) _____
   − 18 °C (0 °F) _____   4 °C (40 °F) _____   27 °C (80 °F) _____
   Difference _____   Difference _____   Difference _____

2. As the temperature increases, the amount of water the air can hold per degree rise of temperature (*increases, decreases, stays the same*). Therefore, as the temperature increases, the saturated vapor pressure increases at (a *geometric*, an *arithmetic*) rate. The amount of water the air can hold at 27 °C (80 °F) is _____ times that at − 18 °C (0 °F).

CONDENSATION

If more water vapor is present than the air can hold, some of this water vapor will condense, or change from the gaseous to the liquid state. Since all air near the surface of the earth contains water vapor, it can be made to yield this water if it can be brought to the saturation point. A parcel of air can be brought to the saturation point if cooled sufficiently, since the ability of air to hold moisture is reduced as the temperature goes down. The temperature at which air will become saturated if cooled sufficiently is known as the *dew point*.

Table 5.1.   Saturation Vapor Pressure Over Water and Over Ice in Millibars[a]

Temperature in °C	Temperature in °C									
	0	1	2	3	4	5	6	7	8	9
40	73.777	77.802	82.015	86.423	91.034	95.885	100.89	106.16	111.66	117.40
30	42.430	44.927	47.551	50.307	53.200	56.236	59.422	62.762	66.264	69.934
20	23.373	24.861	26.430	28.086	29.831	31.671	33.608	35.649	37.796	40.055
10	12.272	13.119	14.017	14.969	15.977	17.044	18.173	19.367	20.630	21.964
+0	6.1078	6.5662	7.0547	7.5753	8.1294	8.7192	9.3465	10.013	10.722	11.474
−0	6.1078 (6.1078)[b]	5.623 (5.6780)	5.173 (5.2753)	4.757 (4.8981)	4.372 (4.5451)	4.015 (4.2148)	3.685 (3.9061)	3.379 (3.6177)	3.097 (3.3484)	2.837 (3.0971)
−10	2.597 (2.8627)	2.376 (2.6443)	2.172 (2.4409)	1.984 (2.2515)	1.811 (2.0755)	1.652 (1.9118)	1.506 (1.7597)	1.371 (1.6186)	1.248 (1.4877)	1.135 (1.3664)
−20	1.032 (1.2540)	0.9370 (1.1500)	0.8502 (1.0538)	0.7709 (0.9649)	0.6985 (0.8827)	0.6323 (0.8070)	0.5720 (0.7371)	0.5170 (0.6727)	0.4669 (0.6134)	0.4213 (0.5589)
−30	0.3798 (0.5088)	0.3421 (0.4628)	0.3079 (0.4205)	0.2769 (0.3818)	0.2488 (0.3463)	0.2233 (0.3139)	0.2002 (0.2842)	0.1794 (0.2571)	0.1606 (0.2323)	0.1436 (0.2097)
−40	0.1283 (0.1891)	0.1145 (0.1704)	0.1021 (0.1534)	0.09098 (0.1379)	0.08097 (0.1239)	0.07198 (0.1111)	0.06393 (0.09961)	0.05671 (0.08918)	0.05026 (0.07975)	0.04449 (0.07124)
−50	0.03935	0.03476	0.03067	0.02703	0.02380	0.02092	0.01838	0.01612	0.01413	0.01236

[a]To find the saturation vapor pressure for 13 °C, read down the left column to 10 °C and across that row to 3 °C. The saturation vapor pressure for 13 °C is 14.969 mb.

[b]Values over water at subfreezing temperatures in parentheses.

PROBLEMS

3. Determine the dew point of the air for the following conditions. (Use Table 5.1.)

Air temperature (°C)	Vapor pressure (mb)	Dew point (°C)
0	4.8	_____
21	14.9	_____
32	36.3	_____
35	37.8	_____

4. Relative humidity is defined as the ratio of the actual vapor pressure of the air to the saturated vapor pressure, expressed as a percentage.

$$\text{Relative humidity} = \frac{\text{actual vapor pressure}}{\text{saturated vapor pressure}} \times 100$$

If the actual vapor pressure of a parcel of air is 25 mb and the air temperature is 29 °C (85 °F) what is the saturated vapor pressure and the relative humidity?

a. Saturated vapor pressure _____

b. Relative humidity _____

5. One of the advantages of technology is being able to live in dwellings that are heated to comfortable temperatures while the temperatures outdoors may be very cold. Bringing cold air indoors and heating it changes its character considerably. Not only is the air heated, but the relative humidity is altered to a great extent.

Air of a temperature of −18 °C (0 °F) and 70% relative humidity is brought indoors and heated to 21 °C (70 °F). What will the relative humidity be indoors? _____ Compare the moisture conditions inside this house with atmospheric conditions at a desert site where air temperature is 38 °C (100 °F) and relative humidity is 12%. Which has the higher absolute humidity? _____ It has been demonstrated that such low humidity inside a house is not only hard on health but also very hard on the structure of the home and on wooden furniture. The wood tends to become brittle and crack. It is recommended that humidity be maintained above 20% and preferably above 40%. For this reason, many modern heating systems incorporate humidifiers.

6. On a clear spring evening the temperature drops at the rate of 1 °C per hour until the dew point is reached. It continues to cool at the rate of 0.5 °C per hour until 6 A.M. If the temperature at 5 P.M. is 10 °C and the relative humidity is 62%, condensation will begin at _____ (A.M., P.M.) in the form of (*dew, frost*) and the minimum temperature will be _____. If the temperature at 5 P.M. is 7 °C and the relative humidity is 57%, condensation will begin at _____ (A.M., P.M.) in the form of (*dew, frost*) and the minimum temperature will be _____.

7. Evaporation is the process of change in state of water from liquid to gas. This is a cooling process, and one means of measuring relative humidity uses this attribute of evaporation. A thermometer with the bulb wetted and with air circulated around it will have a different temperature than one with a dry bulb. The difference in the temperature of the two thermometers is proportional to the relative humidity.

Given the following atmospheric conditions:

Air temperature = 21 °C (70 °F)
Wet-bulb depression = 3 °C (5 °F)

a. What is the relative humidity? (See Table 5.2.) _____

b. What is the saturated vapor pressure of the air? (See Table 5.1.)

_____

c. Knowing the saturated vapor pressure and the relative humidity, calculate the actual vapor pressure of the air.

$$\text{Saturated vapor pressure} \times \frac{\text{relative humidity}}{100} = \underline{\hspace{3cm}}$$

Table 5.2. Relative Humidity

Dry-Bulb Temperature in °C	Depression of the Wet Bulb in °C[a]																			
	1	2	3	4	5	6	7	8	9	10	11	12	13	14	15	16	17	18	19	20
32	93	87	80	74	68	62	57	51	46	41	36	31	27	23	20	16	12			
31	93	87	80	74	68	62	56	50	45	40	34	31	26	22	19	14				
30	93	86	80	74	67	61	54	49	43	38	34	29	25	21	17					
29	93	86	80	73	66	59	53	47	42	37	32	28	24	20						
28	93	86	79	71	65	57	51	45	41	36	32	27	23	18						
27	93	85	78	70	63	56	50	45	40	35	31	26	21							
26	92	84	76	68	61	55	49	44	39	34	30	25								
25	91	82	74	67	60	54	48	43	38	33	28									
24	90	81	72	65	58	52	47	42	37	33										
23	90	81	72	65	58	52	46	41	37											
22	90	81	72	64	58	52	46	41	36											
21	89	80	72	63	57	51	45	40	35											
20	89	80	71	63	57	51	45	39												
19	89	79	71	63	56	50	44	38												
18	89	79	70	62	55	49	44													
17	88	79	70	62	54	48	42													
16	88	79	69	61	54	48														
15	88	78	69	61	53															
14	88	78	69	61																
13	88	78	69																	
12	88	77																		
11	88																			

[a]The depression of the wet bulb is the difference in temperature between the dry thermometer and the wetted thermometer.

d. What is the dew point of this air? (Use Table 5.1.) _____
Note: Dew point is the temperature to which air must be cooled in order for saturation to occur.

e. Determine the relative humidity for each of the following conditions.

Dry-bulb temperature (°C)	Wet-bulb temperature (°C)	Relative humidity (%)
32	30	_____
18	15	_____
16	10	_____

EXERCISE **6**

Adiabatic Processes in the Atmosphere

The primary source for heating of the atmosphere is the surface of the earth. Thus, temperatures in the atmosphere usually decrease with height. This change in temperature with height is referred to as the *lapse rate*.

PROBLEMS

1. The data in Table 6.1 represent the observed temperatures at different heights at two different times of day. Plot the data given in Table 6.1 on Figure 6.1, using a dashed line for the 7 A.M. data and a solid line for the 2 P.M. data. Draw a horizontal line across the graph at the height marking the top of the temperature inversion.

   What factors are responsible for the differences in the two lapse rates that have been plotted?

   The unequal heating of the atmosphere at the surface is one of the factors producing atmospheric turbulence. As air rises from the surface it expands because of decreasing pressure with height. This rate of cooling due to expansion in unsaturated air is approximately 1 °C per 100 m (5.5 °F per 1000 ft). This is called adiabatic cooling because no heat is lost to the system. It is an internal adjustment in energy distribution due to the expanding volume as the air rises.

2. Figure 6.2A represents a parcel of air at the surface with a temperature of 7 °C and a dew point of 2 °C. If the air were to start to rise, it would cool by expansion at the dry adiabatic rate of _____ per 100 m. If the air were to rise until condensation began, the dew point would be reached at a height of _____ m. The altitude at

Table 6.1. Sample Lapse Rates

Altitude (meters)	7 A.M.	2 P.M.
Surface	7 °C	24 °C
360	15	21
720	13	18
1080	11	15
1440	9	12
1800	7	9
2160	5	6

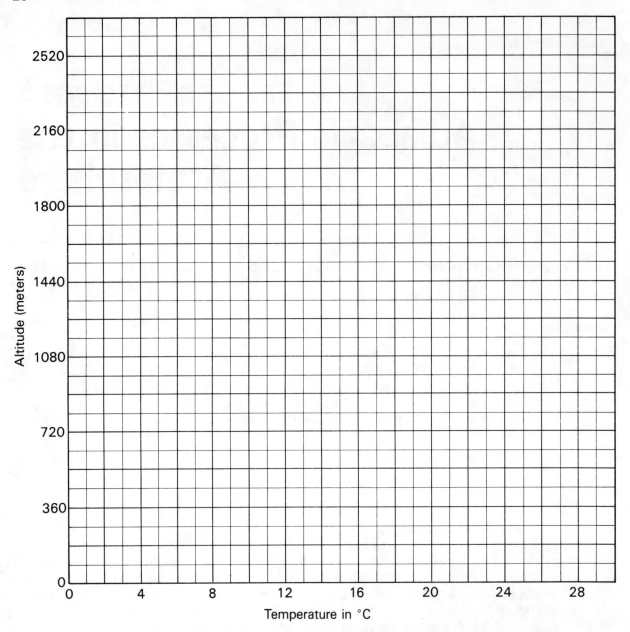

Figure 6.1. **Graphic plot of 7 A.M. and 2 P.M. temperatures**

which the dew point is reached is referred to as the lifting condensation level. This level is often visible in the atmosphere in the form of the flat base of cumulus clouds. In Figure 6.2, point B represents this level in the atmosphere. Insert the altitude and temperature for this level near point B. If the air continues to rise after condensation begins, theoretically it will continue to cool adiabatically at 1 °C per 100 m; however, the condensation of moisture that must occur releases heat into the air at a rate of 600 calories (c) per cm³. (This heat was acquired in the original evaporation of the water.) This addition of heat by the condensation cuts down the net rate of cooling with height. The net rate of cooling while condensation is occurring is known as the wet adiabatic rate. This rate will depend upon how much condensation takes place. The greater the condensation, the lower the net rate of cooling and the lower the wet adiabatic rate. Assume for this problem a wet adiabatic rate of 0.5 °C per 100 m for the parcel of air ascending from B to C. What would be the air temperature at point C? _____

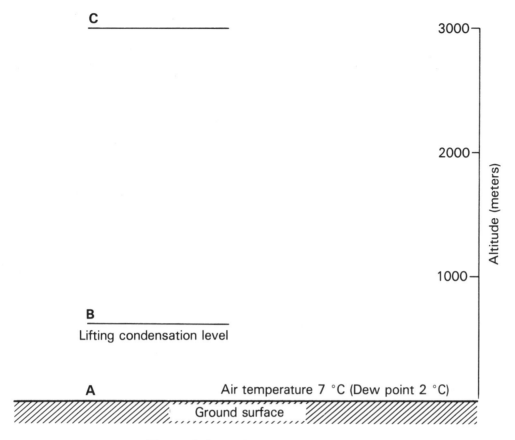

Figure 6.2. Lifting condensation level

If an air parcel descends through the atmosphere the air will heat at the dry adiabatic rate as it will necessarily be unsaturated. Thus while rising air cools at varying rates, descending air heats at a uniform rate. If the parcel of air were to settle back to the surface from level C, the resulting surface temperature would be _____ °C. The parcel of air has been heated _____ °C and the source of the heat was the process of _____ .

Chinook winds serve as a dramatic example of the effects of different adiabatic rates in cooling and heating an air mass. Normally, air rising and flowing over the Rocky Mountains remains aloft downwind from the mountains. However, should the airstream descend the leeward slopes it will warm at the dry adiabatic rate. When the chinook starts to blow in winter, dramatic increases of temperature have been recorded in the area flanking the Rockies in the United States and Canada; for example, in Spearfish, South Dakota, the temperature jumped from −20 °C to 7 °C during a 2-min period on 22 January 1943.

3. On a July day the air temperature at the surface is 32 °C. The wet bulb temperature is 31 °C. There is a broken layer of cumulus cloud present. Using Table 5.2, determine the dew point of the air. The dew point is _____ °C and the cloud base is at _____ m. If the cloud layer is 700 m thick, the temperature at the upper surface of the cloud layer would be _____ °C. (Assume a set adiabatic rate of 0.5 °C.)

EXERCISE **7**
The Seasons—II

Over most of the earth's surface the fundamental aspect of the seasons is not the change in temperature from summer to winter but the alternation of wet seasons and dry seasons. All life forms adjust to the rhythmic pattern of the rainy season and dry season. Throughout the zone from 30 degrees north to 30 degrees south, the change in temperature is small compared to the difference in moisture balance from summer to winter. The continent of Africa illustrates very well the seasonal imbalance in water availability. Table 7.1 contains the mean precipitation for January and July along 20 degrees east from 25 degrees north to 25 degrees south.

PROBLEMS

1. Plot the mean January precipitation on Figure 7.1 using a solid line and the mean July data using a dashed line.

Table 7.1. **Mean Precipitation in Millimeters From 25°N to 25°S at 20°E Longitude**

	Latitude										
	North						South				
Month	25°	20°	15°	10°	5°	0°	5°	10°	15°	20°	25°
July	T[a]	20	120	160	135	90	30	10	T	T	T
January	0	0	T	5	20	50	130	210	260	140	20

[a]T = trace

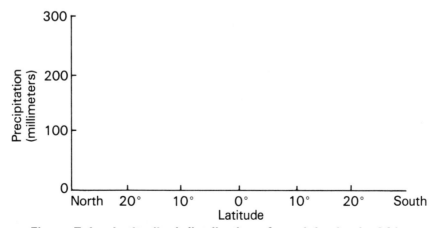

Figure 7.1. **Latitudinal distribution of precipitation in Africa**

Table 7.2. Mean Temperature in °C and Precipitation in Millimeters for Selected Cities[a]

	Jan.	Feb.	Mar.	Apr.	May	June	July	Aug.	Sept.	Oct.	Nov.	Dec.	Year
Denver													
T	0.3	1.4	4.0	9.2	14.3	20.1	23.6	22.8	18.1	12.1	5.1	2.1	11.1
P	12	16	27	47	61	32	31	28	23	24	16	10	327
El Paso													
T	8.1	9.5	13.0	17.8	22.5	28.1	28.3	27.5	24.7	18.5	10.9	7.1	18.0
P	12	10	9	7	10	18	33	30	29	22	8	12	200
Cincinnati													
T	0.9	1.7	5.9	12.3	17.9	23.0	24.9	24.3	20.6	14.4	7.0	1.8	12.9
P	93	71	99	92	97	106	91	83	69	57	75	70	1004
Los Angeles													
T	13.2	13.9	15.2	16.6	18.2	20.0	22.8	22.8	22.2	19.7	17.1	14.6	18.0
P	78	85	57	30	4	2	T	T	6	10	27	73	373
Station _____													
T													
P													
Station _____													
T													
P													

[a]The upper figure in each pair of figures represents temperature and the lower figure represents precipitation.

2. Compare the area under the two curves. Does Africa receive the greater amount of rainfall south of the equator or north of the equator? _____

3. Africa extends over about 70 degrees of latitude. According to the completed graph, what is the width of the latitudinal zone that receives rainfall in both seasons? _____ Most of the continent of Africa experiences a dry season of several months.

SEASONAL DISTRIBUTION OF PRECIPITATION IN NORTH AMERICA

A wide variety of precipitation regimes exists in North America, but four regimes can be established on the seasonal distribution of precipitation. The temperature and precipitation data are given in Table 7.2 for four cities that are representative of the types of regimes. Figure 7.2 shows the areas of the United States that experience each type of regime and the location of the city representing that region. Your instructor may wish to provide in the blank lines in Table 7.2 the data for the city in which you live or some other city.

PROBLEMS

4. Plot the temperature and precipitation data given in Table 7.2 on the graphs provided in Figure 7.3.

5. Which city has the most even distribution of precipitation throughout the year? _____

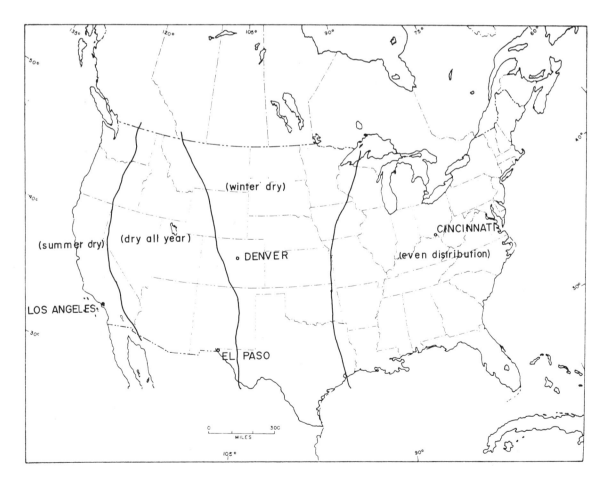

Figure 7.2. Seasonal distribution of precipitation in the United States

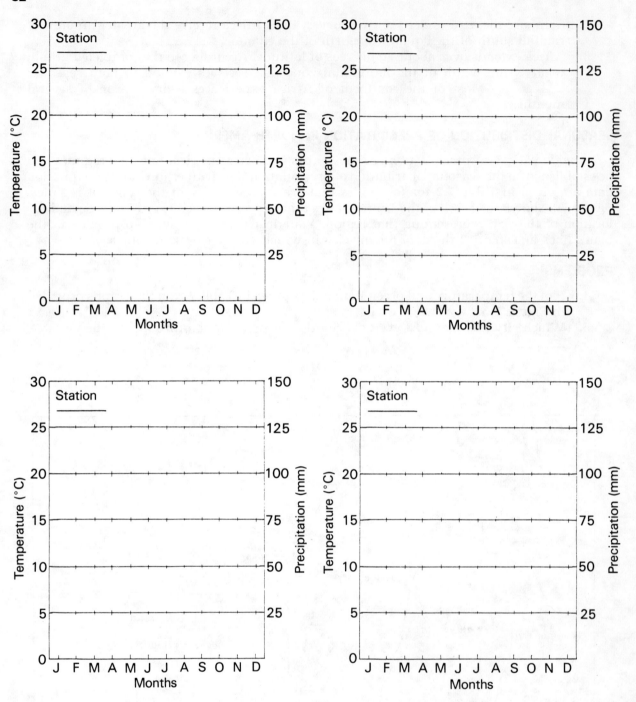

Figure 7.3. Graphs for seasonal variation in precipitation

6. Which city has the greatest share of precipitation in the summer half-year?
   _____

7. Which city has the greatest share of precipitation in the winter half-year?
   _____

8. Deserts are often defined as areas where the average precipitation is less than 250 mm (10 in.). Which of the cities would qualify as a desert city? _____

9. For each of the cities listed below, indicate whether there is a summer dry season (S) or a winter dry season (W), or if the precipitation is spread fairly uniformly throughout the year (f) (use Figure 7.2):

Denver	_____	New Orleans	_____
New York	_____	St. Louis	_____
San Francisco	_____	Omaha	_____
Reno	_____	El Paso	_____
Seattle	_____	Indianapolis	_____

Name: _____

Laboratory section: _____

EXERCISE 8

Probability and Intensity of Precipitation

Precipitation varies widely over the surface of the earth and throughout the year. Deserts are characterized by infrequent and widely scattered rainstorms. Humid areas, such as eastern North America or Great Britain, tend to have frequent precipitation. Two characteristics that provide a great deal of information about the climate of an area are the probability and intensity of precipitation. Probability is a statistical indication of the likelihood of an event occurring in any given period. The probability of precipitation on a given day of the year is expressed thus:

$$\text{Probability (\%)} = \frac{\text{number of rainy days}}{\text{number of days in the year}} \times 100$$

For example, London experiences an average of 164 precipitation days a year. The probability of precipitation on any given day is:

$$\text{Probability} = \frac{164}{365} = 45\%$$

It is for this reason that London has the reputation of being such a rainy place. It rains about every other day. Another site, Cherrapunji, India, has a similar probability. The average number of rainy days is 159 for a probability of 44%.

The frequency of precipitation tells only part of the story. Another aspect of the precipitation in an area is how much precipitation occurs with each event. Intensity of precipitation is a measure of the amount of precipitation per unit time.

$$\text{Intensity} = \frac{\text{total precipitation}}{\text{number of units of time}}$$

If the example of daily intensity is used, the data needed are mean annual precipitation and the number of days with precipitation. London averages 25 in. of precipitation per year.

$$\text{Intensity} = \frac{25 \text{ in.}}{165 \text{ days}} = 0.15 \text{ in./day}$$

Cherrapunji, India, averages 425 in. of precipitation each year, so intensity is considerably higher.

$$\text{Intensity} = \frac{425 \text{ in.}}{154 \text{ days}} = 2.76 \text{ in./day}$$

Cherrapunji gets nearly 20 times as much precipitation in each event. The very low intensity of precipitation in London contributes to the image of a cloudy, drizzly city. It is not a place where a visitor should expect long periods of sunshine.

PROBLEMS

Table 8.1 contains the amount of precipitation that occurred on each day during a year at French Lick, Indiana.

Table 8.1. Daily Precipitation at French Lick, Indiana
(inches)

Date	Jan.	Feb.	Mar.	Apr.	May	June	July	Aug.	Sept.	Oct.	Nov.	Dec.
1	.04	.60				.31						
2	.02		.32	.87	.02	.01					.04	
3	.07	.12	.18	.02		.92			.89		.31	.01
4	.02		.42	.01		.30	.03	.92	.13		.27	
5			.41			.33			.60			
6						.29						
7												
8		.33								.11		
9		.23					.38	.06		.35		
10		.06			.09		.05		.20	1.27	.32	
11	.08				.10			.03				
12	.02				.48					.03		.48
13			.13	.59		.47			.14	.24		
14		.10		.04	.65	.07			.48	1.57		
15		.15	.01		.17	.40			.48	.15	.40	
16					.55	.03						.62
17	.06				.26	.36						.49
18	.01		.40									
19				.75			.22		1.25			
20				.54			.07	1.77		.40	.82	
21				.32		.03				.06		.47
22		.06									.02	.39
23	.07			.08			.05		.04			
24				2.12			.39					
25				.05		.19			.20			
26		.52										
27							.85		.75			
28				.68			.15			.03	.02	
29	.48		.08	.32						.91		
30					.18						.01	
31					.05		.90					

1. Carefully determine the number of rain days in each month and the total for the year.

      Jan. Feb. Mar. Apr. May June July Aug. Sept. Oct. Nov. Dec. Year

    ___ ___ ___ ___ ___ ___ ___ ___ ___ ___ ___ ___ ___

2. Calculate the mean probability of precipitation on any given day of the year.

$$\text{Probability} = \frac{}{365} \times 100 = \underline{} \%$$

3. Calculate the average interval between precipitation episodes.

$$\text{Mean interval} = \frac{\text{number of nonrain days}}{\text{number of intervals between episodes}}$$

$$\text{Mean interval} = \underline{} \text{ days}$$

4. Determine the probability of precipitation on a given day in April. Calculate the probability in December.

5. Calculate the amount of precipitation in each month and for the year. What is the average precipitation intensity in inches per day for the year? _____
6. In which month does precipitation fall most intensely? _____
   What is the mean intensity for the month? _____
7. In which month is precipitation of lowest intensity? _____
   What is the average intensity? _____
8. How can you explain the difference in intensity between these 2 mo?

EXERCISE 9

Wind Systems and Windchill

Wind is the result of pressure differences in the atmosphere and represents the movement of air to restore equilibrium in the system. Winds, or atmospheric circulation, serve two major functions in the environment: to transfer energy from low to high altitudes and to transfer moisture from the oceans to the land masses. Both functions are major ones in the operation of the earth's environmental system.

PROBLEMS

1. A graphic device for illustrating the average wind conditions at a given location is the wind rose. A wind rose is a means of depicting the frequency and velocity with which the wind blows from different directions.

   On Figure 9.1 are the basic outlines for constructing wind roses with the major compass points marked. Complete the wind rose for the 2 mo as follows, using the wind data for French Lick, Indiana, shown in Table 9.1.

   a. Construct lines perpendicular to the circle proportional in length to the frequency with which the wind blows from each direction. Let 1 mm represent each percentage point.

   b. Indicate the average velocity the wind blows from each direction by attaching flags on the direction arrow according to the Beaufort scheme shown in Appendix B, part 9.

   c. In the center of each wind rose, write in the percent of time the wind is calm in each of the 2 mo.

July   January

Figure 9.1. Outlines for wind roses

**Table 9.1. Wind Direction and Velocity for
French Lick, Indiana, in the Months of July and January**

	Direction (degrees)								
	0	45	90	135	180	225	270	315	calm
July									
Average velocity (mph)	10	8	5	5	7	6	8	9	
% of time	2	2	10	14	24	22	12	9	5
January									
Average velocity (mph)	12	7	5	6	8	10	11	14	
% of time	10	2	2	7	10	22	19	18	1

HUMAN PHYSIOLOGY AND WEATHER

A wide variety of factors besides actual temperature determine an individual's sensation of warmth or cold. One of the major factors is wind velocity. In midlatitudes in winter, and in polar areas, winds have a significant effect on the human body and hence on the amount of clothing that must be worn to protect oneself from the cold. The heat loss from the body depends on a variety of factors, such as the amount of the body covered by clothing, the thickness of the clothing, and the amount of physical activity. Normally in cold weather only the face or face and hands would be exposed, accounting for some 3–10% of the surface area of the body. However, when the legs are uncovered, the percentage of exposed surface increases to some 30% or more. An average layer of winter clothing will have a resistance to heat loss of about 1 c/m²/sec compared to 0.5 c/m²/sec for gloves or shoes and, of course, none for uncovered flesh. An additional source of heat loss is through the lungs, and it is very difficult to prevent this kind of heat loss. In fact, as much as 20% of the total heat loss of the body may occur in this fashion. Some of the heat loss is caused by the evaporation of water in the lungs and some by direct heating of the air. The cold air that is breathed in is heated to body temperature and the humidity increased almost to the saturation level.

EFFECTS OF WIND ON COMFORT

In calculating the effective temperature due to windchill, one must take into account that the wind speeds most people experience are usually less than those reported at weather stations. This is because the wind speed increases rapidly away from ground level, being about double at 33 ft above the ground what it is at 1.5 ft. For a person some 5 ft 6 in. tall, the wind velocity is about .57 of reported wind velocity. An exception to this rule, of course, is when wind velocities are reported calm. A person walking at the rate of 3 mph would have an effective wind speed of 3 mph in still air.

The windchill factor increases as wind velocity increases and the temperature decreases. When heat loss becomes significant, injury may occur to the skin on the exposed areas, such as hands, feet, ears, nose, or even legs. In the table of values of windchill (Table 9.2), there are certain critical values which are of interest. For instance, at K = 1400, exposed flesh will freeze, and at K = 2000, exposed flesh freezes in approximately 1 min.

The windchill factor, or cooling due to wind, can be expressed as

$$K = (91.4 - T)(4\sqrt{v} + 5 - v/4)$$

where K = windchill in kilocalories per square meter per hour
T = temperature in degrees F
v = wind velocity in miles per hour

Table 9.2. Sensible Temperature Scale for Various Values of Windchill Factor K

50	Hot
100	Warm
200	Pleasant
400	Cool
600	Very cool
800	Cold
1000	Very cold
1200	Bitter cold
1400	Exposed flesh freezes
2000	Exposed flesh freezes in 1 min
2500	Limit of tolerance

PROBLEMS

2. For the following wind and temperature conditions, determine whether or not the windchill is sufficient to cause frostbite.

Temperature (°F)	Wind (mph)	Frostbite Potential
20°	36	
10°	36	
0°	16	
−10°	9	
−20°	4	

Would any of the cases listed above be sufficiently severe to cause almost instantaneous tissue damage (damage in less than 1 min)? _____ If so, under which set of circumstances?

_____

3. Table 9.3 contains equivalent temperatures based on wind effectiveness and the various rates of heat loss from covered and uncovered portions of the body.

a. Utilizing the table, determine the equivalent temperature when there is an ambient air temperature of 22 °F and wind velocity of 20 mph.

_____

b. If the air temperature is 12 °F, what wind velocity is necessary to produce an equivalent temperature of 0 °F? _____

c. On a given day there is a 35-mph wind and a windchill of 0 °F. What is the ambient temperature? _____

Table 9.3. Windchill Equivalent Temperature in Fahrenheit Based on Clothing Requirements

Temperature (°F)	Wind Speed (mph)								
	Calm	5	10	15	20	25	30	35	40
32	34	32	27	24	21	17	14	12	10
30	32	30	25	21	18	15	12	10	7
28	30	28	23	19	15	12	9	6	4
26	28	26	21	17	13	9	6	3	1
24	26	24	19	14	10	7	3	0	-3
22	25	22	16	12	8	4	1	-3	-6
20	23	20	14	9	5	1	-2	-6	-9
18	21	18	12	7	2	-2	-5	-9	-13
16	19	16	10	5	0	-4	-8	-12	-17
14	17	14	8	2	-3	-7	-12	-16	-20
12	15	12	6	0	-5	-10	-15	-23	-24
10	13	10	4	-2	-8	-13	-18	-26	-28
8	11	8	1	-5	-11	-16	-21	-30	-32
6	9	6	-1	-7	-13	-19	-24	-34	-36
4	7	4	-3	-10	-16	-22	-28	-38	-40
2	5	2	-5	-12	-19	-25	-31	-42	-44
0	3	0	-7	-15	-22	-28	-35	-46	-49
-2	1	-2	-10	-17	-25	-31	-39	-50	-54
-4	-1	-4	-12	-20	-28	-35	-42	-54	-58
-6	-3	-6	-14	-22	-30	-38	-46	-59	-63
-8	-4	-8	-16	-25	-33	-41	-50	-63	-67
-10	-6	-10	-19	-28	-36	-45	-54	-68	
-12	-8	-12	-21	-30	-39	-48	-58		
-14	-10	-14	-23	-33	-42	-51	-62		
-16	-12	-16	-26	-36	-45	-55	-66		
-18	-14	-18	-28	-38	-49	-59			
-20	-16	-20	-30	-41	-52	-63			
-22	-18	-22	-32	-44	-55	-66			
-24	-20	-24	-35	-47	-58				
-26	-22	-26	-37	-49	-62				
-28	-24	-28	-39	-52	-65				
-30	-26	-30	-42	-55	-68				
-32	-27	-32	-44	-58					
-34	-29	-34	-47	-61					
-36	-31	-36	-49	-64					
-38	-33	-38	-51	-67					
-40	-35	-40	-54	-69					

From R. G. Steadman, 1971, "Indices of windchill of clothed persons," *Journal of applied meteorology*, 10: 678.

Name: _____

Laboratory section: _____

The Water Balance

The water balance of a region consists of the precipitation that falls on the land, the evaporation and transpiration processes that return water to the atmosphere, and the runoff in the form of streams that ultimately lead to the ocean. Figure 10.1 contains the annual inflow and outflow of water in these various processes for the United States. Atmospheric inflow represents the atmospheric moisture carried onto the continent by winds from the ocean—both in the form of liquid water in clouds and as water vapor. Atmospheric outflow is the moisture carried off the continent over the national boundaries, also as water vapor or clouds. Surface outflow is the water carried to the ocean by rivers and streams.

PROBLEMS

1. In Figure 10.1 outflow must equal inflow. How many millimeters of water are contained in the surface outflow? _____

2. Also in the water balance, outflow from the land in the form of runoff and evaporation must equal the inflow from precipitation. How many millimeters of water precipitate over the land? _____

3. What percentage of the precipitation that falls over the land goes back to the atmosphere as evapotranspiration? _____

4. What percentage of the moisture that is carried onto the land by the atmosphere is carried away in the same fashion? _____

5. Based on the data in Figure 10.1, only _____ % of the water transported over the United States actually becomes part of our streams.

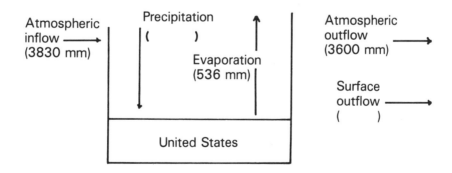

Figure 10.1. Water balance for the United States

The data for the water balance of the United States is a generalization for a large area and the year. It hides a great deal of temporal and spatial variation. Table 10.1 contains data for four different cities in the United States for each month of the year. The first row of data for each city is the potential evapotranspiration (PE). Potential evapotranspiration is the amount of water that would be removed from the surface depending on the temperature. The higher the mean temperature of the month, the greater the potential is for evapotranspiration. The second row is the actual precipitation (P). The third row (AE) is the actual evapotranspiration.

PROBLEMS

6. For each city determine whether there is a moisture surplus or deficit for each month. There is a surplus (S) if precipitation exceeds actual evapotranspiration, and there is a deficit if actual evapotranspiration exceeds precipitation. In the row marked S-D indicate the number of millimeters of surplus or deficit. Indicate a deficit by placing the number in parentheses.
7. Which one of these cities has the most months with a water deficit?

8. Which of the four cities has the greatest cumulative deficit for a dry period (a series of consecutive months with a deficit)? _____
9. Which one of the cities has the greatest annual surplus?

10. All four cities show a surplus for the year. Which city has the smallest annual margin of precipitation over actual evaporation?

11. Southern Florida has a substantial annual surplus of precipitation over evaporation. However, virtually all of the surplus occurs in September and October. Another element in the rainfall of southern Florida is that the large amount of precipitation in September and October falls partly because hurricanes occur most frequently during these 2 mo. In most years rainfall is much less than the average would indicate.

PRECIPITATION AND STREAMFLOW

The U.S. Geological Survey, in collecting, storing, and analyzing data, organizes the data in what is called the water year. The data (Table 10.2) for 2 yr of flow on Clear Creek in central Indiana reflect the seasonal pattern of small streams in eastern North America. Note that in both years the stream dropped to its lowest levels in September and October. For this reason the USGS uses a water year extending from October to September rather than the calendar year. Thus, the water year begins and ends when flow is usually low. The 1984 water year covers the period from October 1983 through September 1984.

PROBLEMS

12. Why does the lowest flow in Clear Creek most often occur around 1 October? Use the climatic data in Table 10.1 for information.

13. How much precipitation fell during the 1980 water year? _____
14. How many millimeters of water ran off the watershed during the 1980 water year?

Table 10.1. Water Balance Data in Millimeters for Selected Cities

	Jan.	Feb.	Mar.	Apr.	May	June	July	Aug.	Sept.	Oct.	Nov.	Dec.
Bloomington, Indiana												
PE[a]	0	0	18	47	92	130	154	136	96	52	16	0
P	96	77	121	95	105	101	100	98	83	82	80	89
AE	0	0	18	47	92	129	145	125	91	52	16	0
S-D	96					(28)						
Miami, Florida												
PE	52	52	78	98	135	159	169	164	144	116	76	56
P	70	53	65	82	172	179	156	159	227	235	72	50
AE	52	52	78	97	135	159	169	164	144	116	76	56
S-D												
Augusta, Georgia												
PE	13	18	38	69	119	159	178	158	115	62	35	14
P	99	108	114	81	78	116	129	124	91	64	67	87
AE	13	18	38	69	117	151	163	145	104	62	35	14
S-D												
Lincoln, Nebraska												
PE	0	0	9	47	88	131	156	139	92	48	10	0
P	16	24	31	64	103	108	98	89	74	50	29	19
AE	0	0	9	47	88	130	147	125	85	48	10	0
S-D												
Station _____												
PE	____	____	____	____	____	____	____	____	____	____	____	____
P	____	____	____	____	____	____	____	____	____	____	____	____
AE	____	____	____	____	____	____	____	____	____	____	____	____
S-D	____	____	____	____	____	____	____	____	____	____	____	____

[a]PE = potential evapotranspiration; P = precipitation; AE = actual evapotranspiration; S-D = surplus or deficit.

Table 10.2. Precipitation and Runoff in Millimeters for Clear Creek

	Jan.	Feb.	Mar.	Apr.	May	June	July	Aug.	Sept.	Oct.	Nov.	Dec.
						1979						
Precipitation	97	81	91	33	86	79	234	112	33	46	41	41
Runoff	74	61	91	36	23	15	33	15	8	8	8	10
						1980						
Precipitation	28	13	229	53	58	66	137	94	13	8	48	25
Runoff	13	10	178	36	19	10	11	10	5	T	T	T

15. The equivalent of how many millimeters of precipitation was returned to the atmosphere by evaporation and transpiration during this water year? _____

16. How many millimeters of water could be expected to be returned to the atmosphere during this year, based upon potential evapotranspiration? (Use the data for Bloomington, Indiana.) _____

Name: _____

Laboratory section: _____

Köppen System of Climatic Classification

After early attempts by the Greeks, no major effort was made to classify climates until the twentieth century. During this interval, however, scattered efforts were made to collect data pertaining to the atmosphere. Perhaps the best-known system of climatic classification at the present time is that by Vladmir Köppen of Austria (1846–1940). His classification is based essentially on the distribution of vegetation. His assumption was that the type of vegetation found in an area is closely related to temperature and moisture. General relationships were already known when Köppen's classification was produced, but Köppen attempted to translate the boundaries of selected plant types into climatic equivalents. The Köppen system is based on monthly mean temperatures, monthly mean precipitation, average annual precipitation, and mean annual temperature.

Köppen recognized four major temperature regimes, one tropical, two midlatitude, and one polar. After identifying the four regimes he assigned numerical values to their boundaries (see Table 12.1). The tropical climate was delimited by a cool-month temperature average of at least 18 °C. This temperature was selected because it approximates the poleward limit of certain tropical plants. The two midlatitude climates are distinguished on the basis of the mean temperature of the coolest month. If the mean temperature of the coolest month is below −3 °C the climate is microthermal, and if the temperature is above −3 °C it is mesothermal. The fourth major temperature category is the polar climate. The boundary between the microthermal and polar climates was set at 10 °C for the average of the warmest month, which roughly corresponds to the northern limit of tree growth.

The system has been subjected to criticism from two aspects. There is no complete agreement between the distribution of natural vegetation and climate. This is to be expected since factors other than average climatic conditions affect the distribution of vegetation. The system is also criticized on the basis of the rigidity with which the boundaries are fixed. Temperatures at any site differ from year to year as does rainfall, and the boundary based on a given value of temperature will change location from year to year. In spite of the criticisms and the empirical basis of the classification, it has proven usable as a general system.

PROBLEM

Table 12.2 contains climatic data for a number of cities in North America. The problem is to classify these cities by climatic type. There are many different ways by which this can be accomplished. Try the following procedure:

1. Polar Climates (E). First determine if the city has a polar climate. Although four of the major climatic types are based partially on temperature, only one is based on

Table 12.1. Major Climatic Types of the Köppen System

Type	Code Letter	Boundary Element
Tropical humid	A	Mean temperature of the coolest month >18 °C
Dry	B	Evaporation > precipitation
Humid mesothermal	C	Mean temperature of the coolest month between −3 °C and 18 °C
Humid microthermal	D	Mean temperature of the coolest month < −3 °C
Polar	E	Warm-month mean temperature <10 °C

Subdivisions of the major classes

Major Type	Subclass 1	Subclass 2	Boundary Element
A	Af		Precipitation in the driest month >60 mm
	Aw		Precipitation in the driest month <60 mm and <100 − r/25. r = precipitation in mm
	Am		Precipitation in the driest month <60 mm but >100 − r/25. r = precipitation in mm
B	BS		r<20t, winter precipitation >70%
			r<20(t + 7), even precipitation distribution
			r<20(t + 14), summer precipitation >70%
			t = temperature in °C
		BSh	Coolest month mean temperature >18 °C
		BSk	Coolest month mean temperature <18 °C
	BW		r<10t, winter precipitation >70%
		BWh	r<10(t + 7), even precipitation distribution
		BWk	r<10(t + 14), summer precipitation >70%
C	Cs		Summer dry; 1 mo with less than 30 mm of precipitation
			One winter month with at least three times driest summer month
		Csa	Warmest month mean temperature >22 °C
		Csb	Warmest month mean temperature <22 °C; at least 4 mo >10 °C
		Csc	1–3 mo >10 °C but <22 °C
	Cw		Winter dry; one summer month with at least 10 times the amount of precipitation as the driest winter month
		Cwa, Cwb, Cwc	The criteria are the same as for Cs climates
	Cf		At least 30 mm of precipitation in the driest month, or does not meet the criteria for Cw or Cs
		Cfa, Cfb, Cfc	The criteria are the same as for Cs climates
D	Df, Ds, Dw		Criteria for f, s, and w are the same as for C climates
		a, b, c	Criteria for a, b, and c are the same as for C climates
		d	Mean temperature of the coldest month below −38 °C
E	Et		Mean temperature of the warmest month between 0 °C and 10 °C
	Ef		Mean temperature of the warmest month below 0 °C

Table 12.2. Climatic Data for Several North American Cities

	Jan.	Feb.	Mar.	Apr.	May	June	July	Aug.	Sept.	Oct.	Nov.	Dec.	Year
Eureka, Northwest Territories (80° 00 N 85° 56′ W)													
	−36[a]	−37	−38	−27	−10	3	6	4	−7	−22	−31	−35	−19
	3	2	1	2	3	3	16	14	11	9	2	2	69
Climatic type _____													
Tanana, Alaska (65° 10′ N 152° 06′ W)													
	−25	−22	−16	−4	8	14	15	12	5	−6	−17	−24	−5
	16	16	13	3	19	31	50	71	45	19	15	16	314
Climatic type _____													
Edmonton, Alberta (53° 34′ N 113° 31′ W)													
	−14	−10	−6	4	11	14	17	16	11	5	−3	−8	3
	24	20	21	28	47	80	85	65	34	23	22	25	474
Climatic type _____													
Vancouver, British Columbia (49° 11′ N 123° 10′ W)													
	3	4	6	9	13	15	18	17	14	10	6	4	10
	139	121	96	60	48	51	26	36	56	117	142	156	1048
Climatic type _____													
Montreal, Quebec (45° 30′ N 73° 35′ W)													
	−9	−6	−2	7	14	19	22	21	16	10	3	−5	7
	87	76	86	83	81	91	102	87	95	83	88	89	1048
Climatic type _____													
Urbana, Illinois (40° 06′ N 88° 14′ W)													
	−2	−1	4	11	17	22	25	24	20	14	5	0	12
	55	53	81	90	107	115	89	77	77	76	67	53	940
Climatic type _____													
Albuquerque, New Mexico (35° 03′ N 106° 37′ W)													
	2	5	8	14	19	25	26	25	22	15	7	3	15
	8	7	13	9	11	12	30	34	14	26	9	13	185
Climatic type _____													
New Orleans, Louisiana (30° 57′ N 90° 04′ W)													
	13	15	17	21	25	28	29	29	27	22	16	14	21
	98	101	136	116	111	113	171	136	128	72	85	104	1369
Climatic type _____													
Key West, Florida (24° 31′ N 81° 47′ W)													
	21	22	23	25	27	28	29	29	28	26	24	22	25
	38	51	44	64	70	102	106	108	166	149	71	43	1012
Climatic type _____													

[a]The upper figure in each pair of figures represents mean temperature in degrees celsius, and the lower figure represents precipitation in millimeters.

temperature alone, and that is the polar climate. Thus it can quickly be determined whether a station represents a polar environment by examining the warm-month temperature. Table 12.1 indicates that to be a polar climate the warm-month temperature must be less than 10 °C. If the city does have a polar climate, determine whether it is a tundra station (Et) or an ice-cap station (Ef) using the criteria in Table 12.1. If it does not meet the requirements of an E climate, go on to step 2.

2. Dry Climates (B). To distinguish among the other climatic types, it is necessary to determine whether the station in question has a dry climate or not. The criteria for classification as an arid climate is the temperature (potential evapotranspiration) and precipitation relationship. Empirically derived relationships have been set up depending upon the seasonal distribution of precipitation. If the major rainfall season comes in the winter, when temperatures are low, it is most efficient. When the precipitation comes primarily in the summer months, it is least effective, because more is lost by evaporation. Here winter is defined as October to March and summer as April to September for the northern hemisphere. For the southern hemisphere these would be reversed, with winter being the 6 mo from April to September. So, to be classified as an arid climate, the data must meet one of the following criteria.

1. If 70% of the precipitation occurs in the winter, then precipitation (in millimeters) must be less than 20t where t equals the mean annual temperature in degrees celsius.
2. If the precipitation is evenly distributed through the year (less than 70% in summer or winter), then precipitation must be less than 20(t + 7).
3. If 70% of the precipitation occurs in summer, then precipitation must be less than 20(t + 14).

The dry climates are further broken down into four categories, depending on the degree of dryness and the temperature regime. If the actual precipitation is less than one half the threshold value, it is considered a desert (B) as against a steppe (BS).

3. Tropical Climates (A). If the data for a station do not meet the criteria for either an E climate or a B climate, it must be a tropical humid climate (A) or a midlatitude humid climate (C,D). If the mean temperature of the coolest month is above 18 °C it is a tropical climate (A). If the mean temperature for any month is below 18 °C, the station has a midlatitude climate and you should go to step 4. There are three major subcategories of the A climates. These subcategories are distinguished by the distribution of moisture through the year. If the precipitation in every month exceeds 60 mm, it is a tropical wet climate (Af). The other two types of A climate each have at least a short dry season, and the difference between the tropical wet-and-dry climate (Aw) and the tropical monsoon climate (Am) depends on the extremes of the wet and dry season. If precipitation in millimeters (r) in the driest month is less than $100 - \frac{r}{25}$, the climate is tropical wet and dry (Aw). If precipitation in the driest month is less than 60 mm but greater than $100 - \frac{r}{25}$, then it is a monsoon climate (Am). The classification of the A climates into subcategories can be simplified by using Figure 12.1. Find the place in the graph matching the precipitation in the driest month and the total annual precipitation, and the climatic type can be read directly from the graph.

4. The Humid Mesothermal and Humid Microthermal Climates (C, D). The humid mesothermal and humid microthermal climates are classified on the basis of the cool-month mean temperature. The humid mesothermal climates (C) have a cool-month average temperature between − 3 °C and 18 °C, and the humid microthermal climates (D), a cool-month average temperature below − 3 °C. There is a wide variety of subcategories, depending on other temperature characteristics and on the seasonal distribution of precipitation. Consult Table 12.3 for criteria for determining the subcategories. Each station should be classified by at least one subclass and two if possible. For example, Greensboro, North Carolina, would be classified as a Cfa climate.

Table 12.4 contains data for a variety of tropical stations, and two blank data sets. Have your instructor provide data for one or two stations and classify them using the Köppen system.

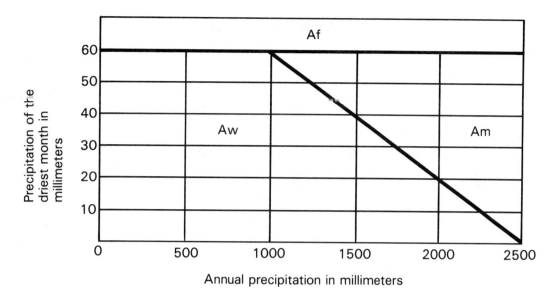

Figure 12.1. Division of tropical humid climates based on seasonal moisture patterns

Table 12.3. Miscellaneous Classes of the C and D Climates

Subclass 3	Criteria
x	Rainfall maximum in late spring or early summer; dry in late summer
h	High frequency of fog
i	Mean annual temperature range less than 5 °C
g	Warmest month precedes the solstice
t^1	Hottest month delayed until autumn
s^1	Maximum rainfall in autumn

Table 12.4. Data for Several Tropical Stations

Jan.	Feb.	Mar.	Apr.	May	June	July	Aug.	Sept.	Oct.	Nov.	Dec.	Year
— Nairobi, Kenya (1° 16′ S 36° 47′ E)												
18[a]	18	19	19	18	16	15	16	17	19	18	18	18
46	51	102	206	160	46	18	25	25	53	109	81	922

Climatic type _____

Iquitos, Peru (3° 19′ S   78° 18′ W)

Jan.	Feb.	Mar.	Apr.	May	June	July	Aug.	Sept.	Oct.	Nov.	Dec.	Year
26	26	24	25	24	23	23	24	24	25	26	26	25
259	249	310	165	254	188	168	117	221	183	213	292	2619

Climatic type _____

Mombasa, Kenya (4° 01′ S   39° 43′ E)

Jan.	Feb.	Mar.	Apr.	May	June	July	Aug.	Sept.	Oct.	Nov.	Dec.	Year
28	28	28	28	26	25	24	24	25	26	27	28	26
30	14	59	192	319	100	72	69	71	86	74	76	1163

Climatic type _____

Kano, Nigeria (12° 03′ N   8° 32′ E)

Jan.	Feb.	Mar.	Apr.	May	June	July	Aug.	Sept.	Oct.	Nov.	Dec.	Year
21	24	28	31	30	28	26	25	26	27	25	22	26
0	T	2	8	71	119	209	311	137	14	T	0	872

Climatic type _____

New Delhi, India (28° 43′ N   77° 18′ E)

Jan.	Feb.	Mar.	Apr.	May	June	July	Aug.	Sept.	Oct.	Nov.	Dec.	Year
14	17	23	29	34	34	31	30	29	26	20	16	25
25	22	17	7	8	65	211	173	150	31	1	5	715

Climatic type _____

Al-Hofuf, Saudi Arabia (25° 15′ N   49° 43′ E)

Jan.	Feb.	Mar.	Apr.	May	June	July	Aug.	Sept.	Oct.	Nov.	Dec.	Year
14	16	21	25	31	34	35	34	32	27	21	16	26
23	8	16	16	1	0	0	T	0	1	1	6	49

Climatic type _____

Station _____

____ ____ ____ ____ ____ ____ ____ ____ ____ ____ ____ ____ ____
____ ____ ____ ____ ____ ____ ____ ____ ____ ____ ____ ____ ____

Climatic type _____

Station _____

____ ____ ____ ____ ____ ____ ____ ____ ____ ____ ____ ____ ____
____ ____ ____ ____ ____ ____ ____ ____ ____ ____ ____ ____ ____

Climatic type _____

[a]The upper figure in each pair of figures represents mean temperature in degrees celsius, and the lower figure represents precipitation in millimeters.

Name: _____

Laboratory section: _____

Interpretation of Aerial Photographs

One of the most effective tools that the physical geographer uses for the interpretation of landforms is the aerial photograph.[1] The benefits of using aerial photographs are many.

When a scene is being viewed through the medium of an aerial photograph, there is an immediate feeling of "naturalness," for the images can be intuitively understood by the observer. This advantage of an air photograph contrasts with the abstract view of the world from a topographic map.

The topographic map is the result of a selective process with symbols representing selected real-world features. Many facets of the landscape have to be omitted; otherwise, the map would be too crowded with information. This selectivity is achieved at the expense of complex reality, which is the forte of the aerial photograph. The complexity of the photograph is balanced by the insights it provides into the real world. Each and every feature that is observed by the camera is recorded.

Aerial photographs do not suffer from problems of human error in the way that maps do, with misplaced symbols, wrongly located roads, and the like.

Aerial photographs for any given part of the United States can be obtained by writing to

The Map Information Office
U.S. Geological Survey
GSA Building
Washington, DC 20242

and in Canada by writing to

National Air Photographic Library
Department of Energy, Mines and Resources
615 Booth Street
Ottawa, Ontario K1A 0E9

THEORY OF STEREOVISION

Aerial photographs are taken with cameras designed for this specific purpose. The aircraft taking the photographs fly along designated *flight lines*, which are parallel but so spaced that photographs from adjacent lines overlap (see Figure 19.1). The overlap between photographs is needed so that stereovision can be attained.

In normal vision, the observer sees objects in three dimensions, namely length, width, and depth. The ability to see depth depends on sight with two eyes, each at an equal distance from the object but viewing it from a different position, or angle. Each eye registers a slightly different image. These images are fused or combined

---

[1]The student wishing to pursue this topic in more depth is referred to T. E. Avery, 1977, *Interpretation of aerial photographs*, 3rd ed. (Minneapolis: Burgess Publishing Co.).

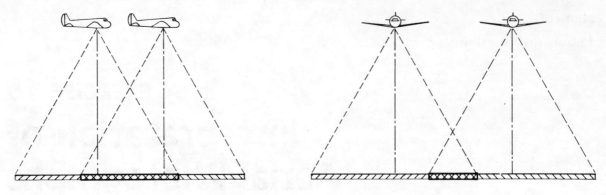

Figure 19.1. Overlap in aerial photographs

by the optic nerves and brain to give depth perception or a third-dimensional view of the object. The distance between the eyes is so short that the angle and difference become so small at great distances that it is difficult to register depth perception.

When viewing two overlapping aerial photographs under the stereoscope, one sees the same ground area from widely separated positions. The right eye is viewing the area in one photograph, the left eye the same area in another photograph. The effect is the same as if a person were viewing the area with one eye located at one camera position and the other eye at the next camera position. The brain so fuses the images that one sees the relief in the photograph, or the third dimension. (USDA, 1951, *Soil survey manual*, Agricultural Handbook No. 18, p. 77.)

AERIAL-PHOTOGRAPH IDENTIFICATION NUMBERS

Not only is the information on the air photograph useful for procuring photographs (because the identification numbers are given), but the date and time (when provided) are most valuable for identifying crops and ground cover, for this information can be linked to the season (Figure 19.2).

THE SCALE OF PHOTOGRAPHS

The scale of an aerial photograph depends on the flying altitude of the aircraft and the focal length of the camera lens (Figure 19.3). The scale of the photograph is therefore

$$S = \frac{f}{H}$$

If the camera has a focal length of 6 in. and the lens is 6000 ft above the ground, then

$$S = \frac{f}{H} = \frac{0.5 \text{ ft}}{6000 \text{ ft}} = \frac{1}{12,000}$$

or, as it is usually written, 1:12,000.

When the photo interpreter faces the situation in which he has no knowledge of the scale of the photograph he is using, then it is necessary to compare the length of a known object on the photograph with the length of the object in reality.

Therefore, the scale of the photograph can be calculated from this ratio:

$$\frac{\text{Length of the object on the photograph}}{\text{Length of the real object}}$$

Unfortunately, this is a difficult technique to apply to photographs that do not have the imprint of human beings on them. Although we have very good ideas about the size of objects made by humans, the size of natural objects is often very difficult to estimate.

The effect of scale on the amount of detail that can be perceived is illustrated by Figure 19.4.

Date　　　　County symbol　　Roll number　　Photograph number

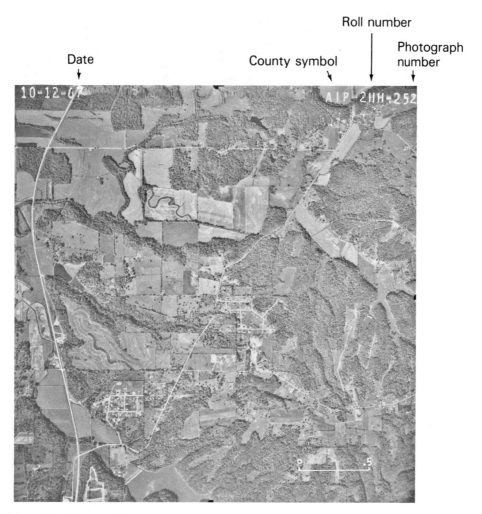

Figure 19.2. Identification numbers on an aerial photograph (USDA, Agricultural Stabilization and Conservation Service)

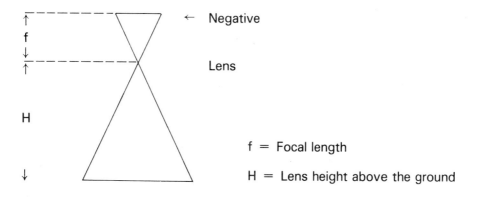

← Negative

Lens

f = Focal length

H = Lens height above the ground

Figure 19.3. Factors determining scale in aerial photography

Figure 19.4. Air photographs of a partly cutover area of ponderosa pine in Arizona. The scales of the photographs are 1:15,840; 1:6000; 1:3000. (U.S. Forest Service)

OBLIQUE AND VERTICAL AIR PHOTOGRAPHS

There are two types of photographs in general use for interpretation purposes (Figure 19.5).

Oblique. Oblique photos can be regarded as the normal view of the earth's surface. In viewing one of these photographs there is immediate recognition of the scene that is photographed.

Vertical. A vertical angle is more difficult to comprehend because it is only very rarely that a person views an object in the plan view. For this reason maps have been dealt with first in the manual so that a feeling for the vertical photograph is gained from the "vertical" topographic map. The map is nothing but a stylized vertical view of the world.

USEFUL PROPERTIES OF AERIAL PHOTOGRAPHS

Whereas maps have symbols with an established meaning, aerial photographs have different tones and patterns, which must be distinguished and given a meaning by the interpreter.

Size. In using this property of an object, the photo interpreter must use an object or shape that is recognizable and from this absolute size he or she can place the other objects into their relative size brackets. For example, most commercial buildings can be distinguished easily from single-family residences by size alone (Figure 19.6).

Shape. Of all the properties in this list, shape is frequently the factor that provides the key evidence for the interpreter. This is especially the case with respect to landform interpretation, where the external form of a feature is its identifying mark. With features formed by humans, shape can be puzzling as frequently as it can be illuminating, because we are so used to viewing objects from a side view rather than a plan view.

Tone. This property of a photograph is a result of the different light reflectivity of the surfaces that compose the earth's crust. With black and white photography, tone is expressed by differing degrees of grayness (white and black colors occur, though not very frequently). No feature has a constant tone, for this will vary with the reflectivity of the

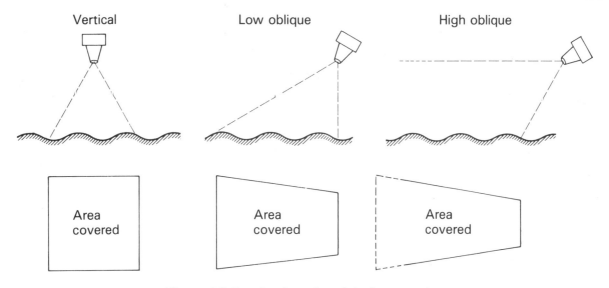

Vertical   Low oblique   High oblique

Area covered   Area covered   Area covered

Figure 19.5.   Angles of aerial photography

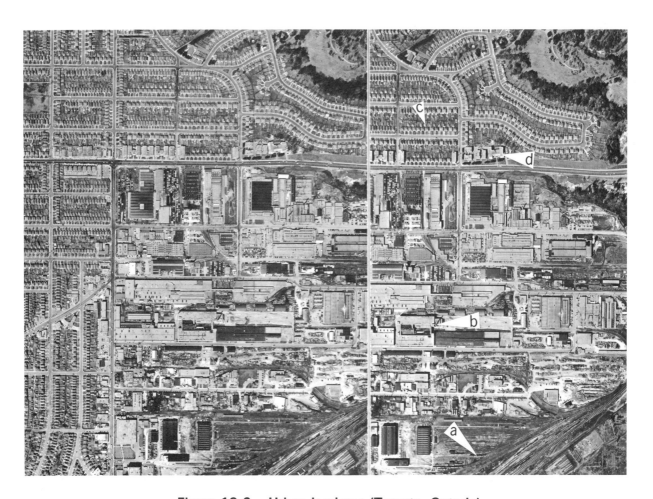

Figure 19.6.   Urban land use (Toronto, Ontario)

object, the weather, the angle of light on an object, and moisture content of the surface. For example, water can be either black or white, depending upon the angle of the sun's rays and the camera's view.

The sensitivity of the response of tone to all the aforementioned variables makes it a very discriminating factor. Slight changes in the natural landscape are more easily comprehended because of tonal variations. The forest comes across as a complicated but rich source of information; the differing tones illustrate the species, canopy types, and age of vegetation.

Pattern.   The spatial distribution of man-made or natural objects is frequently a vital clue to their identity. Excellent aids are those systematic and orderly patterns such as orchards, housing subdivisions, or waves on a lake. The arrangement or pattern of glacial features like drumlins, moraines, and outwash plains also can be a critical factor in deciphering the landforms of a region.

Texture.   This is a difficult property to describe, but it is essentially a way of characterizing the smoothness or coarseness of the image on the photograph. Texture involves the total sum of tone, shape, pattern, and size, which together give the interpreter an intuitive feeling for the landscape he is analyzing. This property is not one that can be defined accurately but is nevertheless vital to the understanding of aerial photographs.

EXAMPLES OF AERIAL PHOTOGRAPHY

Figures 19.7–19.15 illustrate a variety of natural and artificial landscapes. Examine each photograph with an awareness of the properties described in the previous section.

PROBLEMS

1. Discuss two situations (with your reasons) where aerial photographs are less useful than maps.

    a.

    b.

2. You are given the following information about an aerial photograph
    Focal length of the camera = 10 in.
    Flight altitude   = 15,000 ft
    What is the scale of this photograph (expressed as a representative fraction)?

3. Identify the features at the very tip of the arrows in Figure 19.6:
    a.
    b.
    c.
    d.

4. The people who settled the area in Figure 19.14 were French. Where in the United States would you expect to find such a pattern of long lots and long linear fields?

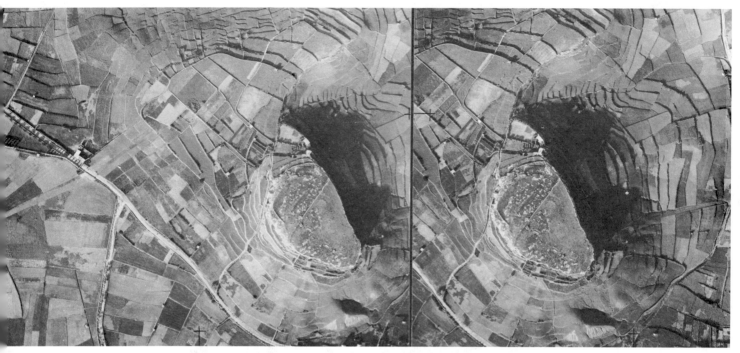

Figure 19.7.   Terraced farming in a dry climate (Malta)

Figure 19.8.   Football stadium and surrounding parking lots in Bloomington, Indiana (USGS)

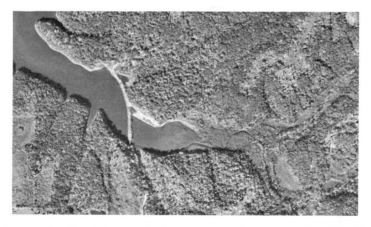

Figure 19.9.   Forested slopes around a reservoir (USGS)

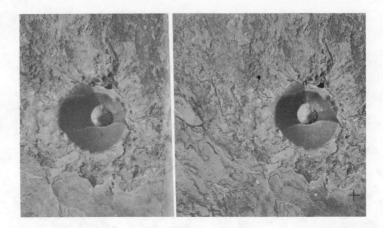

Figure 19.10. Cinder cone (Stikine Plateau, British Columbia) (Department of Energy, Mines, and Resources, Ottawa, Ontario)

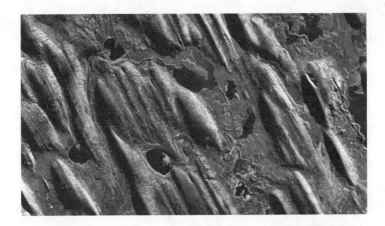

Figure 19.11. Drumlins and eskers (Athabasca Plain, Saskatchewan) (Department of Energy, Mines, and Resources, Ottawa, Ontario)

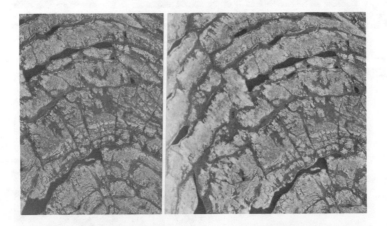

Figure 19.12. Folded rocks—a portion of a dissected anticline (Labrador) (Department of Energy, Mines and Resources, Ottawa, Ontario)

Figure 19.13. Residential land uses (USGS)

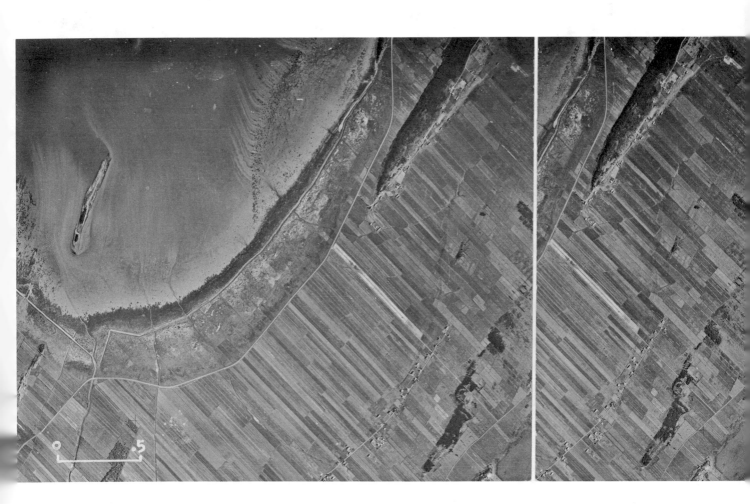

Figure 19.14. Rural land use along the St. Lawrence River in Quebec (1:34,684) (Geological Survey of Canada, A11660—290 and 291)

Figure 19.15. Okanagan Valley near Penticton, British Columbia (Department of Lands, Forests, and Water Resources, Victoria, British Columbia)

5. The linear village in the lower part of Figure 19.14 is located on an advantageous physical site. Explain.

6. The Okanagan Valley scene (Figure 19.15) is a complex rural and low-density residential landscape. After studying the photograph, answer the following questions:

   a. What are the three major types of transportation in this area?

   b. What kind of agriculture is carried on here?

   c. How has the river been modified?

7. Illustrated in Figure 19.13 are different types of residential development. You can predict from the photograph which housing will be more expensive to buy. What evidence can you obtain from the photograph to support this assertion?

8. The left-hand side of Figure 19.7 has a fine example of the benefits of shadow in photo interpretation. Find the example and describe what you are probably looking at.

Name: _____

Laboratory section: _____

EXERCISE *20*

Landforms Reflecting Geologic Structure

Although most of the landform exercises in this manual deal with the impact of different external processes (glaciers and water, for example) on the landscape, it must always be kept in mind that many landforms have a component that is in no way related to subaerial processes but rather is the effect of structure.

In a strict, geologic sense the term *structure* applies to the breaks and geometric shapes of rock bodies such as:

Anticlines
Normal faults
Monoclines

In physiography, however, structure is used in a way that includes not only folds and breaks in rocks, but also the resistance of given rock bodies to erosion dip and strike of rock joints. Hence, *structure* is a term with both specific and general meanings. By reference to the structure of the geologic units, it is possible to interpret the apparently puzzling surface configuration of the landscape (Figure 20.1).

PROBLEMS

Little Dome, Wyoming (Figure 20.2).   The interaction of lithology, structure, and landforms is often most elegantly expressed in areas where the crust has been folded in a dome, as it has to form Little Dome in Wyoming. The Weald of southeastern England and the Black Hills of South Dakota are other examples of large partially eroded domes.

1. Is this a symmetrical or asymmetrical dome? _____ What is the reason for your answer?

2. Identify two "flatirons" on the photograph. Use a colored arrow to locate them.
3. Draw a diagrammatic topographic section across Little Dome along the *x-y* line.
4. Use a set of ten dip arrows spaced around the dome to show the dip of the rocks. An enlarged version is illustrated:
     This runs parallel to the strike ⟶ ⟋⟍ ———— This points down the dip.

Harrisburg, Pennsylvania (Figures 20.3 and 20.4).

5. Using Figure 20.3 as the guide, identify on the map (Figure 20.4):
    a. Anticline
    b. Synclinal mountain or ridge
    c. Pitching syncline
    Write these terms on the map beside the actual feature.

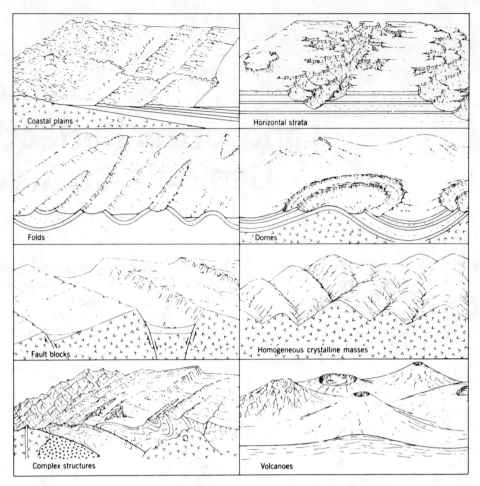

Figure 20.1. Landforms in differing structural situations (From A. N. Strahler, 1969, *Physical geography,* 3rd ed., copyright 1969 by John Wiley and Sons, New York)

6. Explain how the Harrisburg map has been used to support the theory of super-imposed drainage.

7. Make a sketch map of the area covered by the topographic map to include:
   a. All the major rivers
   b. Crest lines of all the ridges
   With this sketch map in front of you, how would you divide the drainage pattern into groups? What would be the reason for your division?

8. Differential erosion of the weak and strong beds shows the tight-fold structure of the Appalachian Mountains very clearly. Using Figure 20.3, color the outcrop of the Pocono and Tuscarora formations on Figure 20.4.

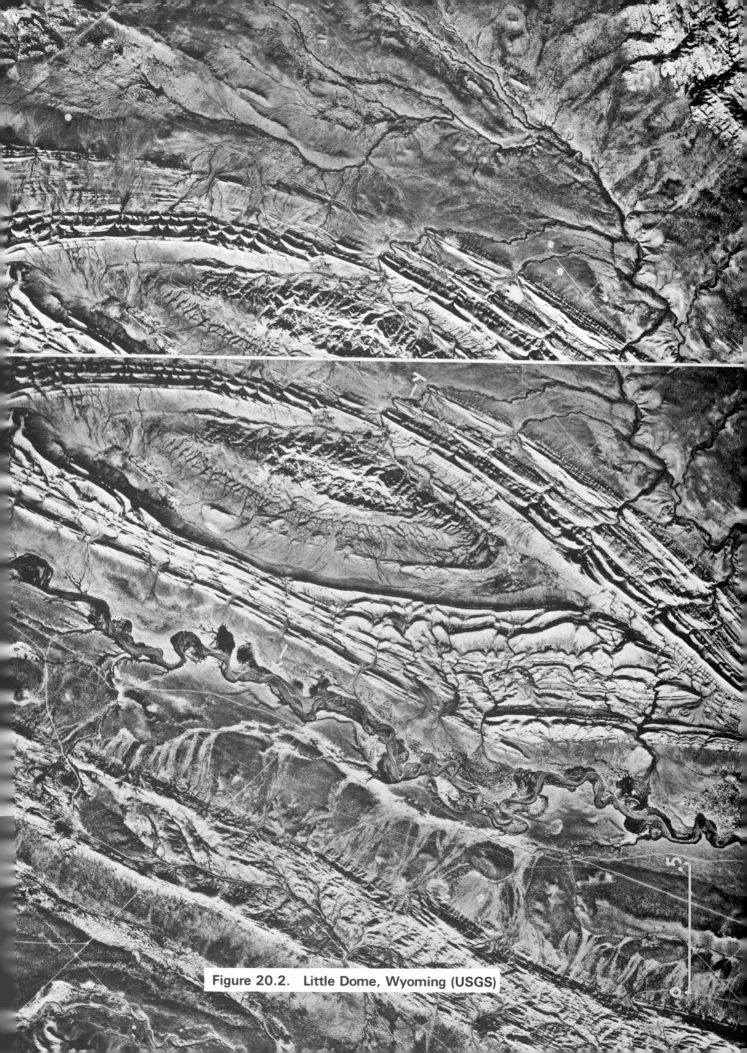

Figure 20.2.   Little Dome, Wyoming (USGS)

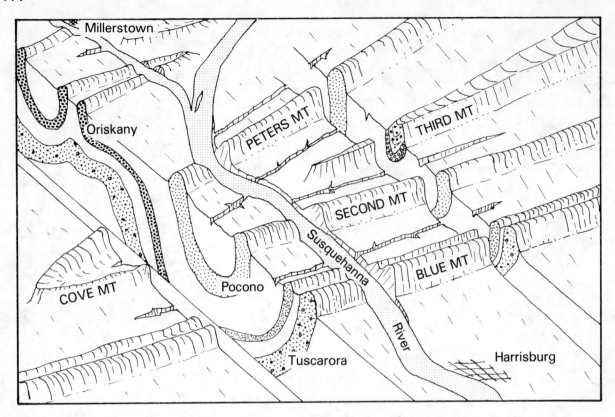

Figure 20.3.   Diagrammatic view of the folded Appalachians near Harrisburg, Pennsylvania. Three of the ridge-forming rock bodies are identified: The Pocono, Oriskany, and Tuscarora groups. (After A. K. Lobeck, 1924, *Block diagrams.* New York: John Wiley and Sons)

9.   What is the relief of Blue Mountain in the area just north of Harrisburg?

Guelb er Richât, Mauritania (Figure 20.5).

10.   The symmetry of the landforms forming the dome is very nearly perfect. (You will observe that the French use very detailed symbols to denote cliffs [scarps] and ridge crests.) Why do you think it is probable that the very center of the dome is composed of igneous rock?

11.   What type of drainage pattern is present? _____
12.   Identify the following landforms on the map (use an arrow with a letter):
   a.   b.

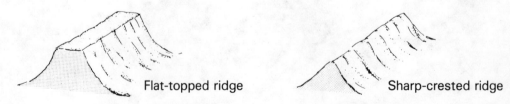

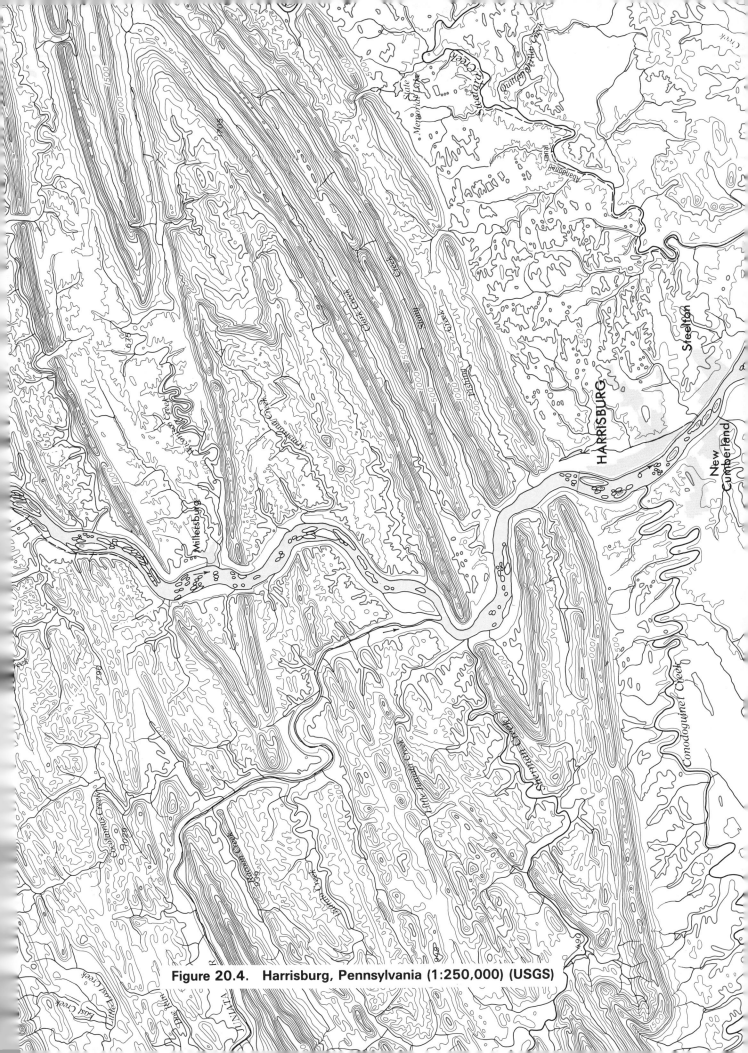

Figure 20.4. Harrisburg, Pennsylvania (1:250,000) (USGS)

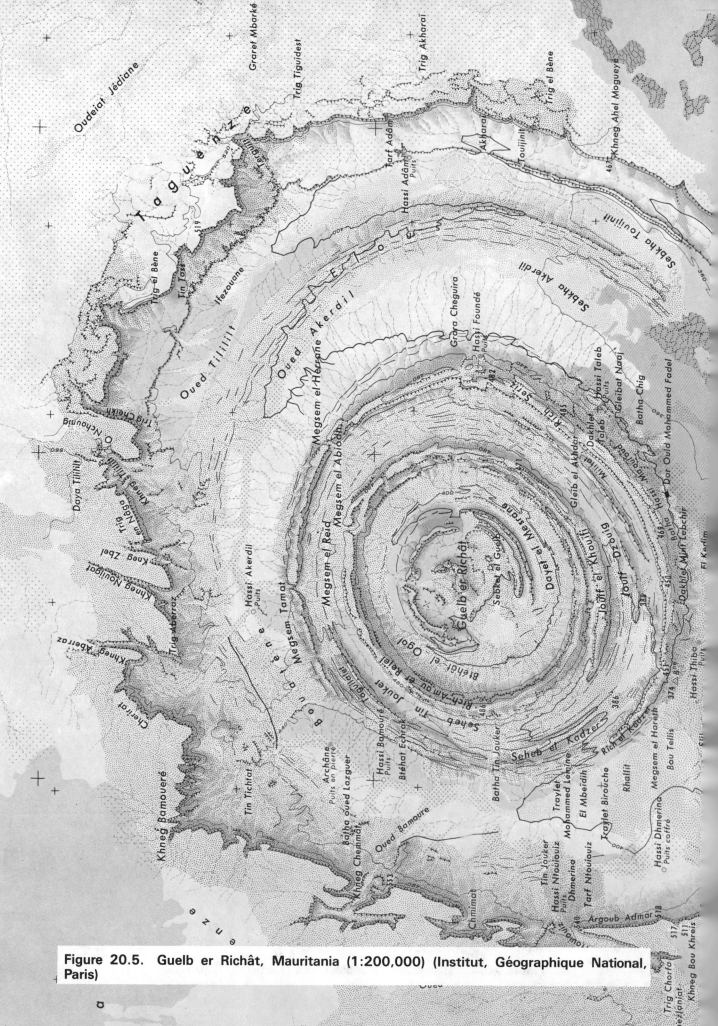

Figure 20.5. Guelb er Richât, Mauritania (1:200,000) (Institut, Géographique National, Paris)

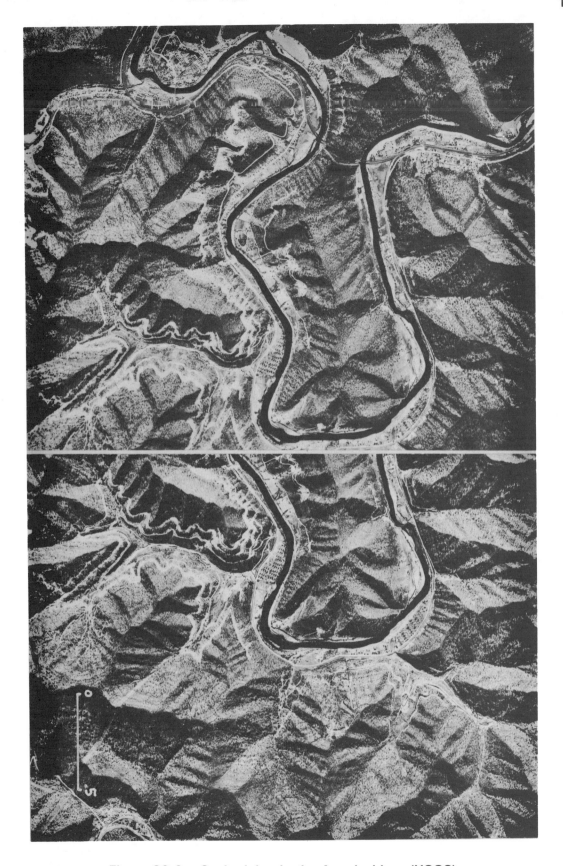

Figure 20.6.   Coal mining in the Appalachians (USGS)

c.

Butte

d.　Wadi (arroyo): a steep-sided valley
typical of arid areas

13.　One indication of the aridity of this area is the care taken to show the occurrence of wells (Fr., *puits*). Mark the location of five wells by using a colored dot.

14.　If you were to stand on the outer rim of the dome, would the central area of Guelb er Richât be at approximately the same elevation as you are, or much lower?

_____

15.　Figure 20.6 has indirect evidence of structure, which in this case refers to the dip of the beds.

a.　What are the white crenulated lines that follow the valleys?

b.　Do these lines closely follow the contours? _____

c.　What is the dip of the beds? (Give a qualitative, not quantitative, answer.)

d.　Is there evidence of more than one coal seam? _____

Name: _____

Laboratory section: _____

EXERCISE **21**

Volcanic Landforms

Clear proof that the earth is an active, living planet is provided by the numerous zones of volcanic activity scattered over its surface. Areas of crustal weakness, associated with mountainous areas like the Rockies and the Himalayas, are the places where volcanic activity is largely concentrated.

A convenient method of classifying volcanic landforms is that based on whether the *magma* cooled within the crust or on the earth's surface:

Intrusive volcanic forms	**Extrusive volcanic forms**
Dikes	Central vent volcanoes
Sills	Cinder cones
Batholiths	Calderas
Laccoliths	Volcanic plugs

Before working on this exercise, review in your textbook the section on volcanic activity.

PROBLEMS

Menan Buttes, Idaho (Figure 21.1).

1. Suddenly rising out of the Snake River floodplain in Idaho are twin cones, the Menan Buttes. The following questions help to define the dimensions of the features:

    a. What is the relief of the buttes? (To define the base of the cones, use the 4850-ft contour line; for the top of the cone use the highest elevation on the rim.)

    South cone: _____ ft
    North cone: _____ ft

    b. What is the depth of depression at the top of the south cone? (To define the top of the depression, use the highest elevation on the rim.) _____ ft.

2. What does the jumbled, chaotic topography in the northwest corner of the map represent?

3. Why do you think these cones are relatively recent (in terms of geological age)?

Des Chutes River, Oregon (Figure 21.2).   Some of the most extensive volcanic regions on the earth's surface have been formed, not by central-vent volcanoes, but by the

Figure 21.1.   Menan Buttes, Idaho (1:24,000) (USGS)

Figure 21.2. Basic lava flows exposed by the downward cutting of the Des Chutes River, Oregon (Oregon State Highway Department)

outpourings of huge volumes of basaltic lava from fractures in the earth's crust. These fractures are referred to as linear-vent volcanoes.

4. The outpouring of lava in the Columbia River Plateau was such that we can observe today several lava beds superimposed one upon another. What evidence is there from Figure 21.2 to support the preceding statement?

5. What has happened to the topography in Figure 21.2 that existed before the lava flows?

6. There is evidence of landslides in Figure 21.2. Indicate landsliding on the photograph by outlining with a colored pencil the area involved.

Country adjacent to Spanish peaks, Colorado (Figure 21.3).

7. What volcanic features formed the ridges near Spanish Peaks?

Figure 21.3. Country adjacent to Spanish Peaks, Colorado (1:20,000) (USGS)

8. Are these features *more* or *less* resistant than the rock into which they are injected? What reason would you give for your answer?

9. Study the features in Figure 21.3 carefully and decide which system of ridges is *younger* (you can identify a particular system by its trend).

Mount Capulin, New Mexico (Figure 21.4).

10. Mount Capulin is a *scoria* cone (scoria is a relatively fine volcanic ash—4 mm to 32 mm in diameter) that has suffered very little erosion. Given that scoria is very permeable and this is an area of semiarid climate, how would you explain the lack of erosion?

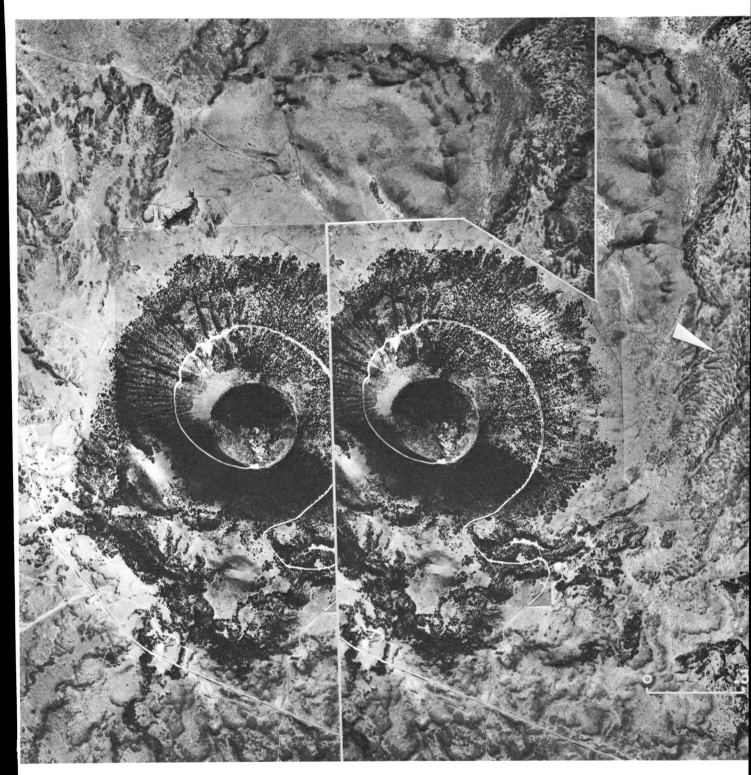

Figure 21.4.   Mount Capulin, New Mexico (1:20,000) (USGS)

11. Aside from the well-preserved cone, there is another clear volcanic feature on Figure 21.4 (the arrow points to it).

    a. What is it, and what evidence is there that it was once flowing?

    b. Put an arrow on the photograph to show the direction of flow.

12. What type of drainage pattern is evident on the cone? (Examine Figure 22.3 before answering this question.) _____

13. What is the diameter of the cone at its base (to the nearest 0.1 mi)? _____

Mount Pagan (Figure 21.5).
14. The dominant feature of Figure 21.5 is Mount Pagan, a basaltic lava cone located within the remnants of a caldera. Identify and discuss what the arrows are pointing towards:

    a.

    b.

    c.

    d.

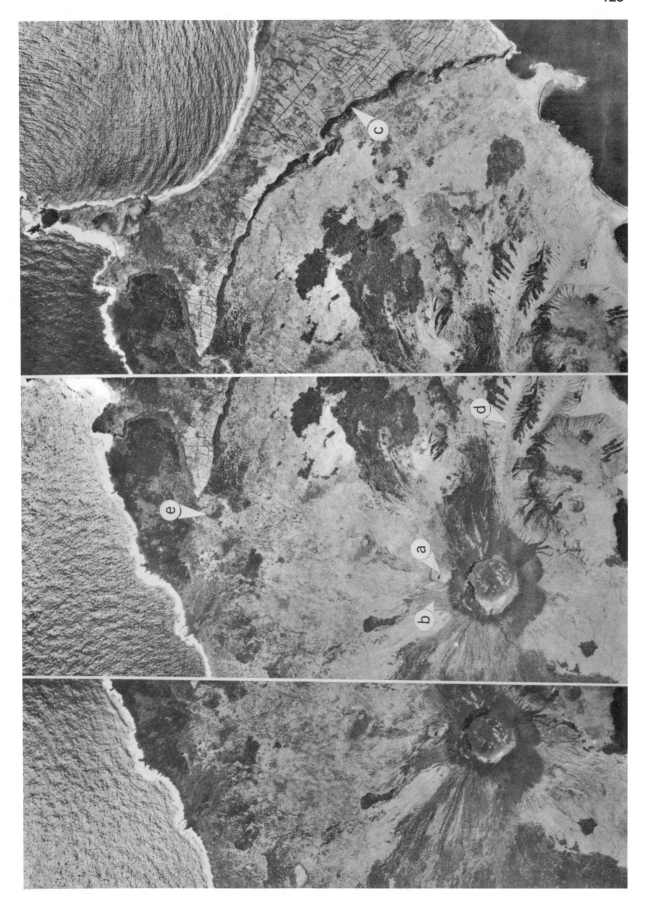

Figure 21.5. The volcanic cone of Mount Pagan, Mariana Islands (1:30,000) (USGS)

Name: _____

Laboratory section: _____

EXERCISE **23**
Fluvial Landscapes

To achieve any level of real understanding about the evolution of the earth's landscapes and human settlement thereon, one must have an appreciation of the effects of water as an agent of environmental change. Historically, human dependence on water has been shown clearly by the emergence of the so-called hydraulic civilizations on floodplains such as those of the Nile, Tigris-Euphrates, and Ganges. In North America, the flat slopes and rich soils of floodplains are areas of productive agriculture.

One of the most comprehensive attempts to order and explain fluvial landforms was made by American geographer William Morris Davis. His theory of landform development was based on evolutionary principles; he called it the "geographical cycle." Depending on the degree of dissection, a landscape can be classified using this theory into youthful, mature, and old-age stages of the cycle.

Review the following in your textbook:

Meanders and meander belts

Point bar deposits

River terraces

Levees

Yazoo-type streams

River rejuvenation

Selected features of a river landscape are illustrated by Figure 23.1:

  a Meandering stream
  b River terrace scarp
  c Point bar deposits
  d Oxbow lake
  e Deposition on the inside of a meander

PROBLEMS

Beatton River, British Columbia (Figure 23.2).

1. Is the Beatton River at a high- or low-water level? Support your answer with evidence from the figure. _____

2. There is clear evidence in the stereo pair in Figure 23.2 to show the stages in the abandonment of an oxbow. Marking the photograph, where appropriate, explain the preceding statement.

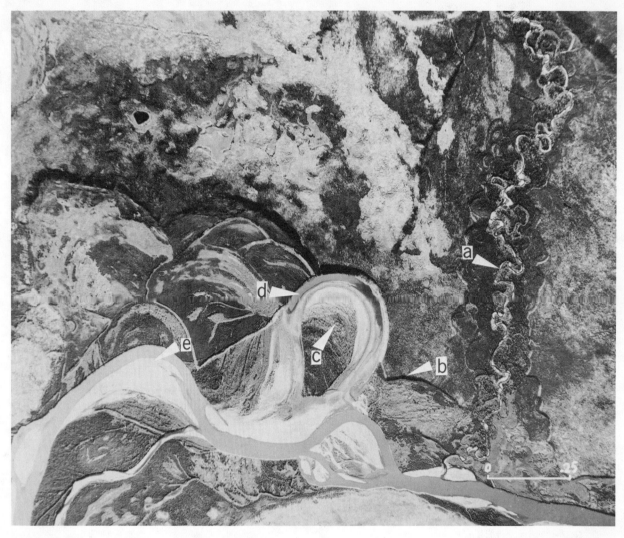

Figure 23.1. Stewart River, Yukon Territory. See the text for an explanation of a-e. (Geological Survey of Canada, 99666)

3. What is the name of the feature that marks the progressive migration of a meander? _____. With a colored pencil, indicate by an arrow an area on the photograph with such features.
4. There is some indication that part of the area covered by the stereo pair is *outside* of the meander belt. Indicate where it is on the photograph.

Saint Mary River, Alberta (Figure 23.3).

5. What evidence is there that the Saint Mary River has been rejuvenated?

6. Using a colored arrow, point to an abandoned meander (use the right-hand photograph).

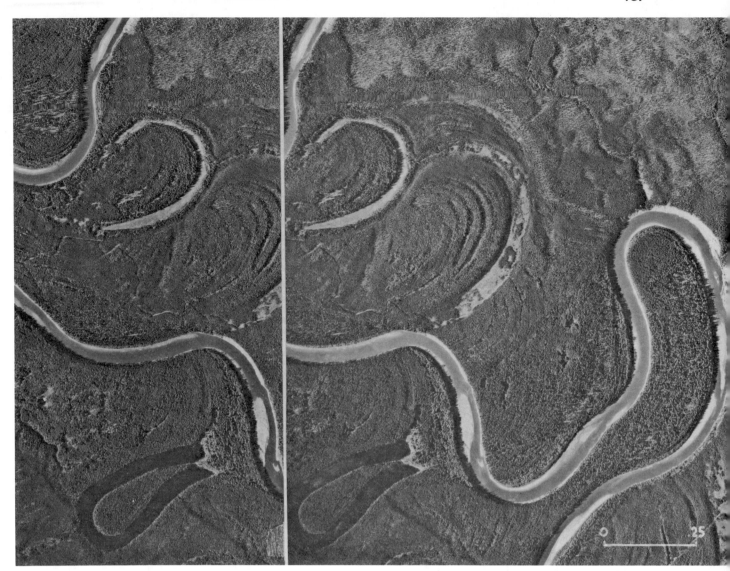

Figure 23.2. Beatton River, British Columbia (Department of Lands, Forests, and Water Resources, Victoria, British Columbia)

    7. Does a, on the photograph, point to a natural mound of rock or one created by humans? Explain your choice.

    8. Climatically, does Figure 23.3 depict an area with high or low precipitation? _____ Cite the evidence for your answer.

Philipp, Mississippi (Figure 23.4).
    9. What is the Matthews Bayou?

Figure 23.3. The floodplain of the Saint Mary River, Alberta (1:22,909) (Geological Survey of Canada, A6722—52 and 53)

10. How would you classify the Tippo Bayou (that is, what kind of stream is it)?

11. What evidence is there that humans have attempted to control the course of the Tallahatchie River?

12. Which way has the meander of the Tallahatchie River, immediately north of Philipp, been moving? _____ Why is the 5-ft contour interval, rather than a 10- or 20-ft interval, especially valuable for topographic map interpretation in this area of the map?

Figure 23.4.   Philipp, Mississippi (1:62,500) (USGS)

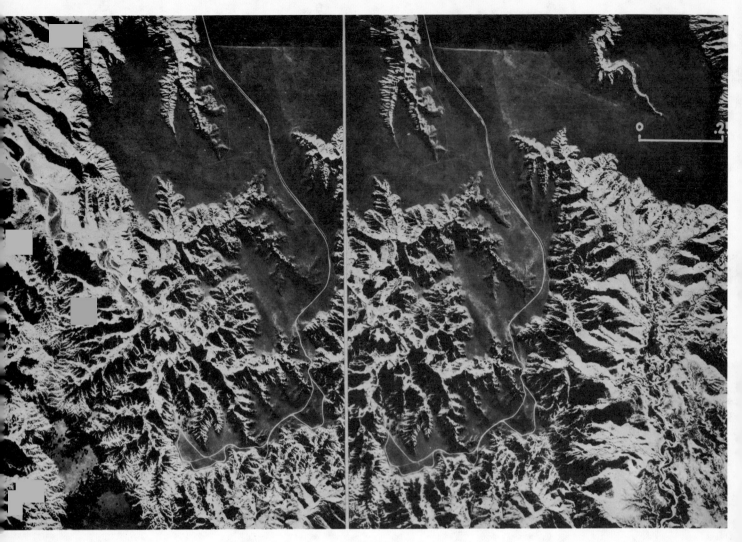

Figure 23.5.   Badlands National Monument, South Dakota (1:17,000) (USGS)

Sheep Mountain Table, South Dakota (Figures 23.5 and 23.6).   The most intricate, deeply gullied landscapes to be found in North America are "badlands," of which the area east of Rapid City, South Dakota, is the most well known. Badlands (Figures 23.5 and 23.6) were produced by a combination of the following:

Impermeable clays and shales
Semiarid climate
Intense thunderstorms
Incision of a major stream

13.   The mesa (Sheep Mountain Table) that is apparent both on the map and in the air photograph is a tableland that is being gradually _____ . What will be the result of the evolution of this landform in the distant future (that is, what will it look like in the geologic future)?

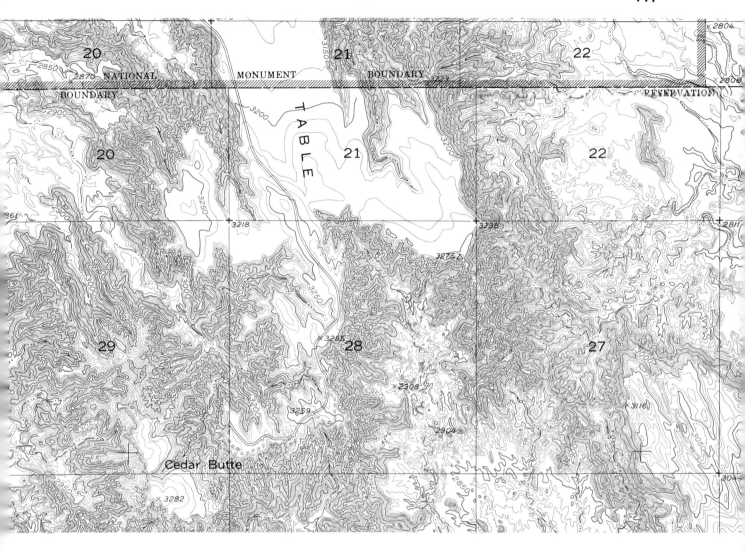

Figure 23.6. Sheep Mountain Table, South Dakota (1:24,000) (USGS)

14. What is the total relief (highest elevation minus lowest elevation) of this map extract (Figure 23.6)? _____ ft.

15. Is this a region of high or low drainage density (exclude the mesa from your answer)? Compare the drainage density in Figure 22.5 before answering this question. _____

16. What parts of the mesa will be most rapidly consumed by erosion in the near geologic future? Use two or three arrows on the map to illustrate your answer.

Name: _____

Laboratory section: _____

Landforms of Limestone Terrain

In areas where limestone is at or close to the surface, a set of landforms and underground features is formed that is distinctive enough to be given the name *karst topography*. Flanking the Adriatic Sea is a belt of limestone terrain, approximately 200 km wide, extending from Albania to the Italian border in western Yugoslavia. This is the region of the Dinaric karst—the classic example of such topography. Other areas of karst include sections of Indiana-Kentucky (Figure 27.1), southern Ontario, northern England, the Cévennes of France, and Puerto Rico.

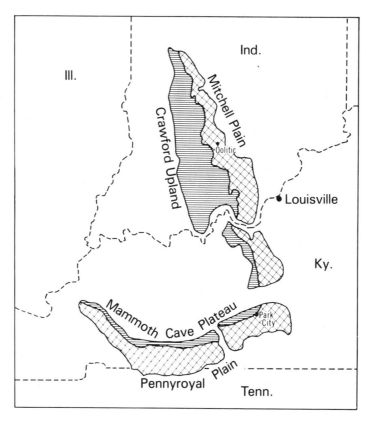

Figure 27.1. The karst areas of Indiana and Kentucky (After W. E. Davies and H. E. LeGrand, 1972, ''Karst of the United States,'' in *Karst,* ed. M. Herak and V. T. Stringfield. Amsterdam: Elsevier Publishing Co., p. 496, Fig. 17)

ELEMENTS OF KARST TOPOGRAPHY

Solution.   The process leading to the development of karst landforms is the solution of limestone. Carbon dioxide will enter into solution with rain and stream waters, increasing their acidity; this increased acidity results in faster limestone solution. When limestone terrains are examined in the field, those places where the limestone is in contact with running water are smooth, reflecting the removal of limestone by solution.

Underground water.   In most areas of the world, karst landscapes are characterized by having very little surface water in the form of streams. Water is able to infiltrate very rapidly into the permeable limestone through surface depressions that will be identified in the next section as *sinkholes*. The water flows underground in caverns that can be very extensive; these underground streams may appear as springs or rises, which are characteristic of karst areas.

Landforms.   The most common landform feature of karst areas is the *sinkhole* (some textbook authors favor the term *doline*), which is the most obvious expression of limestone solution. Sinkholes have dimensions that vary in diameter and in depth from a couple of feet to 100 ft. In general, the sinkhole is best described as a funnel-shaped depression. In places where the water table is high, the sinkholes may contain small lakes or ponds. However, the major function of the sinkhole in the karst landscape is to act as a conduit for surface water to enter the underground passageways and caverns in the limestone.

Where erosion has removed the soil cover over a limestone area, the revealed surface is usually very rugged, with deep grooves, pits, and flutings carved into it. Such a surface is called a *lapies* surface.

In the karst areas of Indiana and Kentucky, many streams have formed *blind valleys*. This condition arises when a surface stream goes underground by way of a doline and the stream valley is terminated by a bluff.

The karst found in tropical humid climates can be put into a separate category, for although sinkholes are present, the landscape has a very different appearance. Erosional remnants are found as individual hills with the intervening limestone largely removed; this is beautifully illustrated by the "tower" karst of Puerto Rico.

THE KARST REGION OF KENTUCKY AND INDIANA

Sections of central Kentucky and southern Indiana are underlain by extensive areas of Mississippian limestone. The spatial relationship of the physiographic regions is given by Figure 27.1.

The Crawford Upland and Mammoth Cave Plateau are equivalent physiographic units, though the Crawford Upland is not so karstified as its Kentucky equivalent.

The Mitchell Plain and Pennyroyal Plain are the most developed karst areas with sinkholes frequent and readily identifiable even on topographic maps.

The Kentucky karst regions are separated by the Dripping Springs Escarpment; there is no equivalent to this in Indiana. Park City, Kentucky, is located directly next to the escarpment.

PROBLEMS

Park City, Kentucky (Figures 27.2–27.4).

1. After studying Figures 27.2 and 27.3, you will recognize that the two physiographic units shown in Figure 27.1 are represented in these figures (Mammoth Cave Plateau and the Pennyroyal Plain). On Figure 27.4, insert the Dripping Springs Escarpment, which is the boundary between the two regions by way of a line like this:

Marking the top of the escarpment

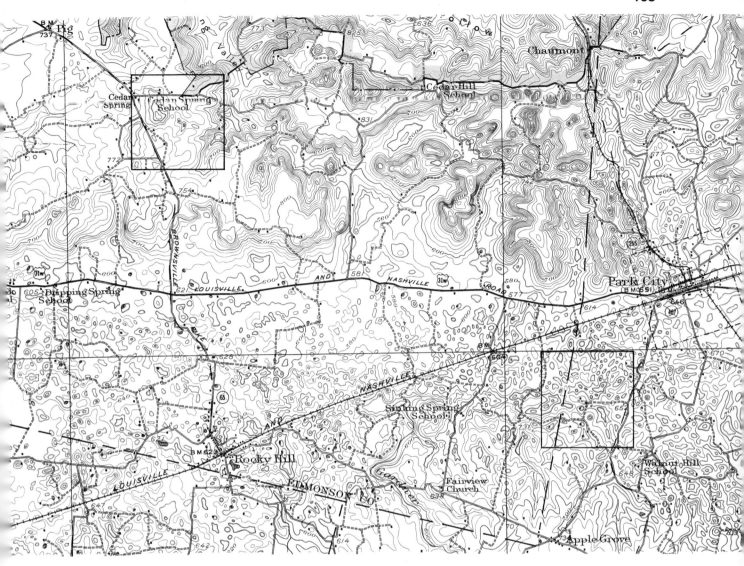

Figure 27.2. Mammoth Cave, Kentucky (1:62,500) (USGS)

After you have done this, write in the name of the physiographic units on the diagram.

2. a. Which physiographic unit has the largest number of sinkholes?

   _____

   b. With the aid of a small arrow, point to an example of a blind valley on the Park City map in Figure 27.2 (use a colored pencil).

3. Describe the differences in density (number per unit area) and morphology of sinks between the Mammoth Cave Plateau and the Pennyroyal Plain. To calculate density, count the number of sinks in the sample squares (quadrats) on the map (Figure 27.2).

4. One of the most sensitive environmental aspects of karst regions is the ease and rapidity with which the groundwater can be polluted. Why should this be so? (Use your knowledge of underground conditions in karst.)

Figure 27.3.   Karst topography west of Park City, Kentucky (1:18,000) (USGS)

5.   Between Chaumont and Park City there is a line of sinkholes. What kind of structural feature would you use to explain this linear trend?

Manatí, Puerto Rico (Figure 27.5).   This stereo pair covers an area some 4 mi west of Manatí, near the northern coast of Puerto Rico.

6.   The solution of limestone is more rapid under warmer temperatures. Which area, Puerto Rico or Indiana, is having its karst terrain more rapidly eroded?

7.   This karst area has a very different look from those in temperate climates.

   a.   The bottom two thirds of the stereo pair is a complex mosaic of sinkholes and sharp ridges. As a sinkhole enlarges, what happens to the ridges?

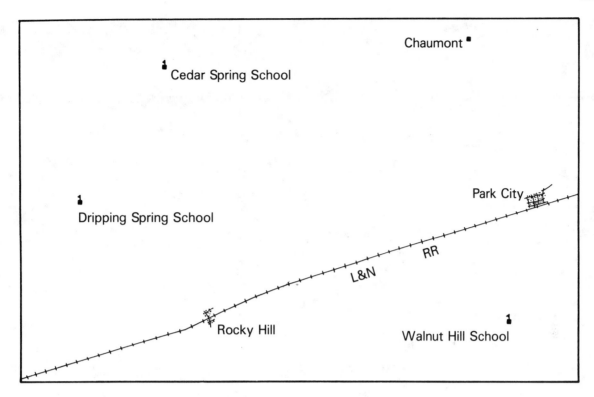

Figure 27.4. Outline map of the Park City area

b. People's use of the sinkhole terrain is fairly intensive. What does the pattern of regularly spaced dots (objects) probably represent?

c. Put an X on the stereo pair where you can find what might be a sinkhole opening.

8. Compare and contrast the temperate area of karst (Figure 27.2 and Figure 27.3) with the tropical karst (Figure 27.5).

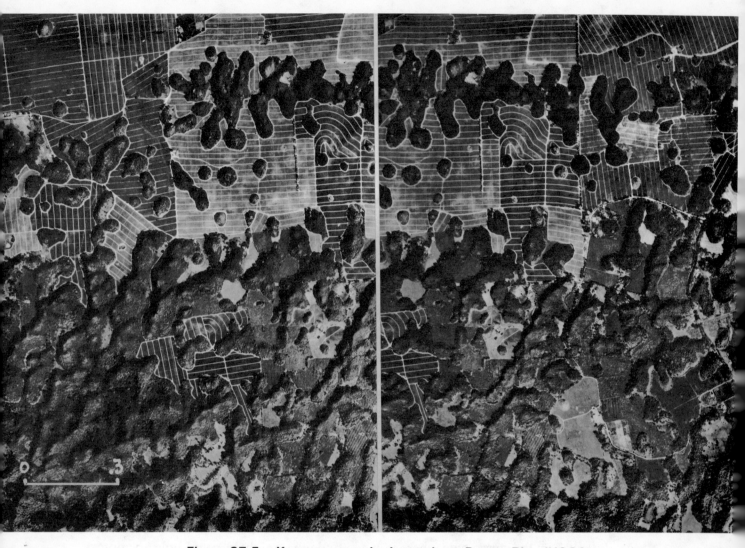

Figure 27.5. Karst topography in northern Puerto Rico (USGS)

Name: _____

Laboratory section: _____

EXERCISE 28

Landforms of Arid Regions— Introduction and Alluvial Fans

Arid climates are prevalent over approximately one third of the earth's land surface (Figure 28.1). Climatically, the world's desert regions are characterized by:

Low rainfalls (and low humidities)

Great rainfall variability—both in terms of time and spatial distribution

High average wind speeds

Intense heating by day and cooling by night

Sparse vegetation (not a climatic factor but listed here for convenience)

This list represents the major *external* elements responsible for the nature of desert land-forms; the structure and lithology of rocks in desert areas are the *internal* elements involved.

Hollywood has promoted the myth of extensive sand dunes typifying desert conditions and implying, at the same time, the efficacy of wind action. However, it is the action of water, strange as it may seem, and not the work of wind that is the prime agent of desert landscape evolution.

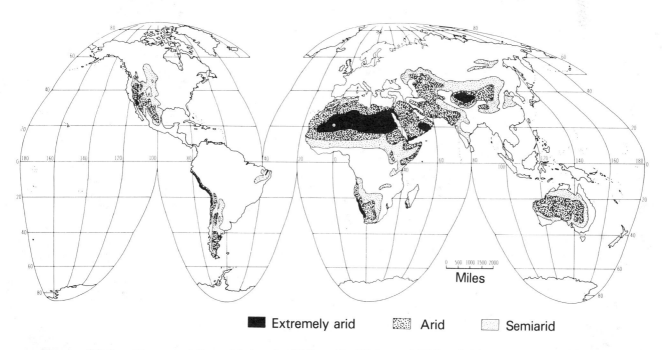

Extremely arid   **Arid**   **Semiarid**

Figure 28.1. The world's arid lands (After P. Meigs, 1953, Arid-zone research paper, UNESCO)

The key to the understanding of the action of water in the desert is its variability, because a place that might have been dry for 25 yr can suddenly be inundated by a very intense thunderstorm. A dry *arroyo (wadi)* will be transformed into the channel of a raging torrent, and in the space of a few hours an amazing amount of erosion and sedimentation will have taken place.

In this and the succeeding exercises the following landforms will be examined: alluvial fans, dunes, and high mountain streams.

ALLUVIAL FANS

In arid areas alluvial fans are found flanking mountain fronts. The traditional explanation for the formation of alluvial fans has been that they formed by deposition caused by the drop in velocity of the stream as it left the mountains and flowed out over the plain. A different view of alluvial fan formation has been put forward, because the previous explanation is inadequate for locations where the stream profile is a smooth one, showing no interruption or break at the mountain front. When water in the stream reaches the mountain front, it has the tendency to spread out and not be confined to well-defined channels. This increase in width is accompanied by a drop in velocity and a decrease in depth; the outcome is that the sediment load is dropped.

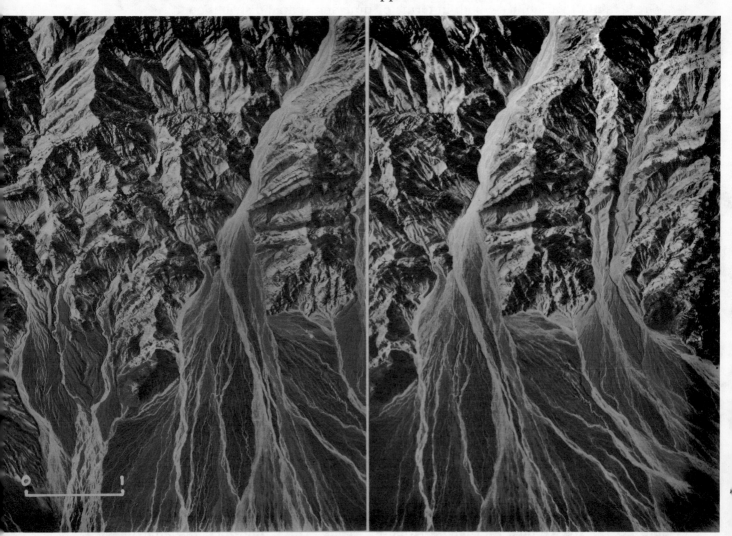

Figure 28.2.   The Trail Canyon alluvial fan on the east flank of the Panamint Range, California (1:60,000) (USGS)

PROBLEMS

1. In what ways is the stereo pair (Figure 28.2) more informative about the surface of the Trail Canyon alluvial fan than the topographic map is (Figure 28.3)?

2. The geologic map of Trail Canyon (Figure 28.4) indicates the changing positions of the stream channels (washes) crossing the fan. (Note: both desert varnish [a coating of iron and manganese oxide on bare rock surfaces] and weathered gravel indicate a lack of movement by water.)
    a. What is there about the pattern of the modern washes to indicate the fanlike spreading of alluvial material?

    b. Where does the alluvial material come from?

3. Does the material forming the Trail Canyon fan come from the watershed high in the Panamint Range or from side slopes or from both sources? Clearly indicate the evidence.

4. Using a colored pencil or black felt-tip pen, insert on Figure 28.3 the limits of alluvial fan sedimentation shown in the left photo of the stereo pair in Figure 28.2.

Figure 28.3. Furnace Creek, California (1:62,500) (USGS)

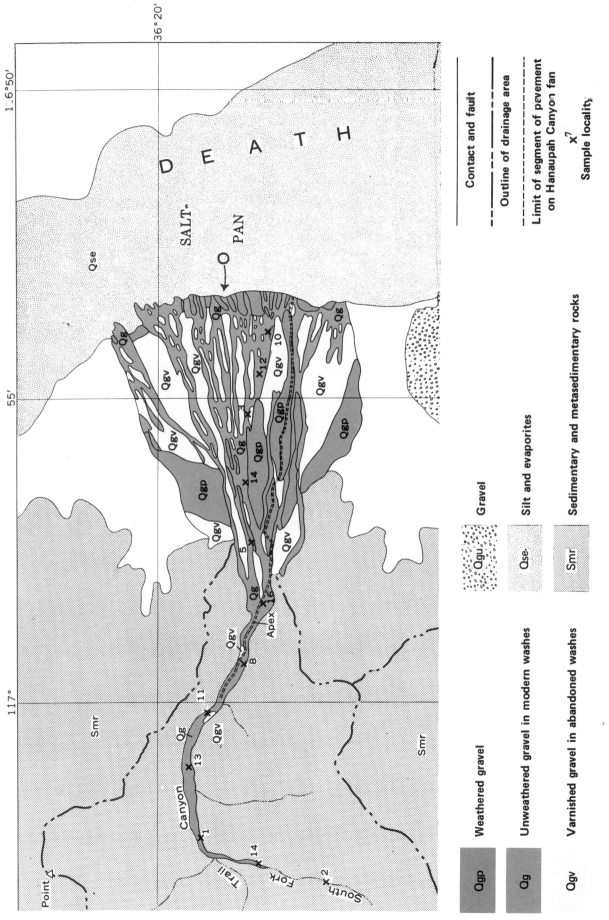

Figure 28.4. Geologic map of Trail Canyon (USGS)

5. Draw a cross section across the Trail Canyon area (as shown on Figure 28.3) from the point △2389 to the bench mark (BM X-252) on the road that skirts the base of the fan.

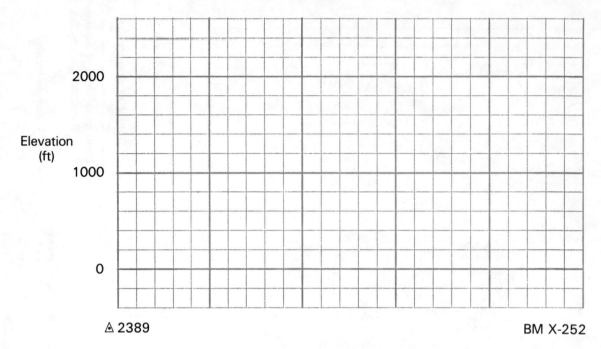

△ 2389   BM X-252

6. What are the potential dangers to urban settlement on alluvial fans?

7. If the processes forming alluvial fans continue, what will happen to the low area of Death Valley?

8. Why should a permanent road avoid an alluvial fan?

Name: _____

Laboratory section: _____

Landforms of Arid Regions—Dunes

Dunes, those transient features of the desert landscape, are the result of a delicate adjustment between:

Wind strength and direction
Sand availability
The nature of the desert surface

From the interaction and balance between these variables there develops a variety of dune types.

OBSTACLE DUNES

Obstacle dunes form when sand collects in the lee of an obstacle (boulder, bush, or cliff) that interrupts the flow of the wind (Figure 29.1).

BARCHAN DUNES

Barchan, or *crescentic*, dunes are located perpendicular to the dominant wind direction wherever they are found (Figure 29.2). The wind direction usually can be ascertained, in that the tips of the barchan dunes extend downwind. Whether these dunes are clustered in interacting groups or scattered individually is a function of sand supply. The greater the sand supply, the less clearly separated are the dunes.

SEIF DUNES

Where sand is piled in long ridges, often extending over many kilometers, then it is termed a *seif*, or *longitudinal*, dune (Figure 29.3). The seif dune is rarely a perfect, symmetrically shaped ridge but is more often one with undulations in the crest line and frequent breaks in the ridge itself. The seif dunes run parallel with the dominant wind direction.

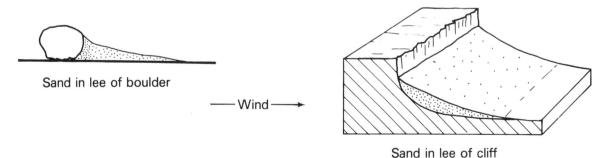

Sand in lee of boulder

— Wind —→

Sand in lee of cliff

Figure 29.1. Obstacle dunes

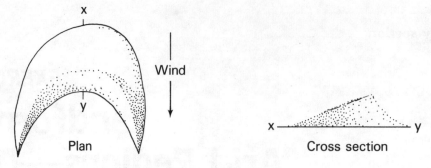

Figure 29.2. A barchan dune

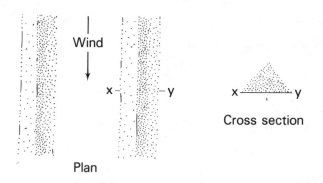

Figure 29.3. Seif dunes

For both the barchan and seif dunes, the location of a given dune is an ever-changing response to sand supply and wind movements. However, as long as there is a steady supply of sand (and a steady wind) the dunes will remain in an area.

PROBLEMS

1. a. Assume that the left-hand side of the air photo in Figure 29.4 is north. What is the direction of the dominant wind in this area? _____ What evidence indicates this wind direction?

    b. Are there any dunes other than barchan dunes shown in this photograph?
        _____

    c. Wind is clearly an important process in modifying this landscape. What other process is obviously at work? _____ What evidence is there of this process?

2. What is the major difference between the barchan dunes of the Peace River area (Figure 29.5) and the ones in California (Figure 29.4)? Describe the response of

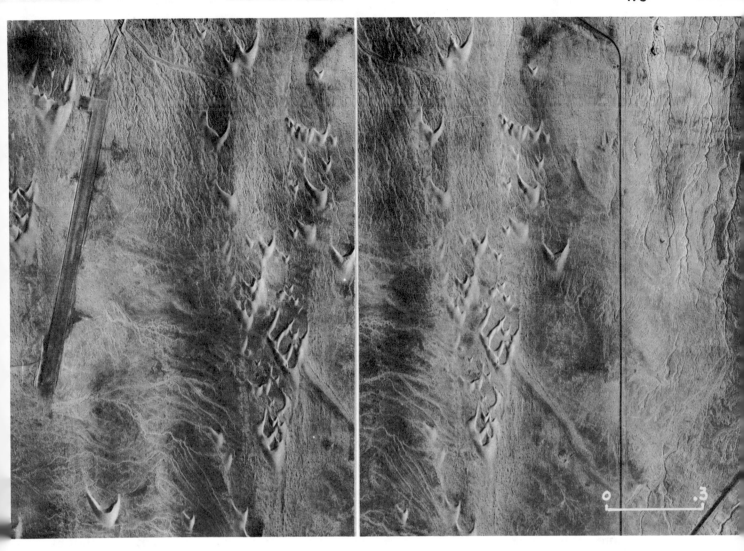

Figure 29.4. Barchan dunes on a plain west of the Salton Sea, California (1:20,000) (USGS)

vegetation to these barchan dunes in Alberta. What factors would you suggest for this response?

3. a. What is the name of the area from which this photograph (Figure 29.6) of longitudinal dunes comes? _____
    Why are these dunes similar, in one sense, to those of a very different shape in Alberta (Figure 29.5)?

    b. The major agricultural enterprise of this area (Figure 29.6) is cattle raising. With this information in mind, observe the areas of erosion (white colors denote

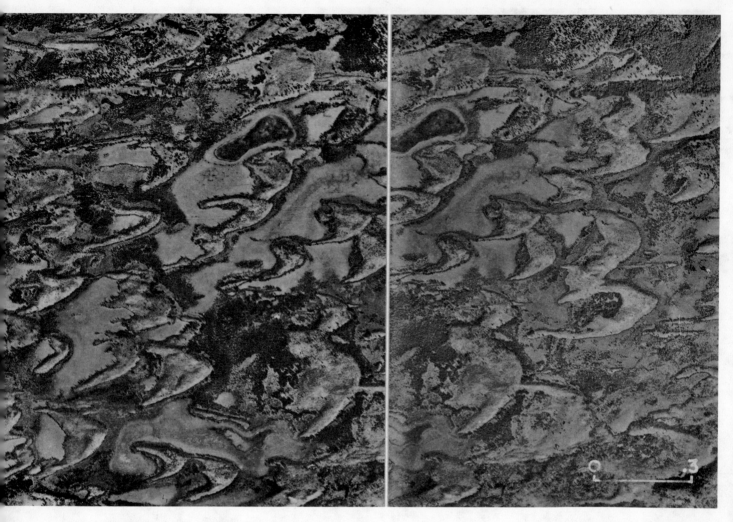

Figure 29.5. Barchan dunes in the Peace River lowland of northern Alberta (1:20,265) (Geological Survey of Canada, A14044—144 and 145)

erosion). Areas of erosion show a pattern (ignore the dunes in the upper portion of the photograph with systematic linear features on them. Describe this pattern and give an explanation.

    c. Assuming the top edge of the photograph is north, what was the direction of dominant wind flow? _____

    d. Do you think there is any justification for calling these dunes fossilized? _____

4. Some areas of dune development are characterized by a lack of definite pattern (Figure 29.7). Check a map of Colorado to determine the geographic setting of these dunes.

    a. Given that the dominant wind is westerly (west is the bottom edge of the stereo pair) how would you explain the location of these dunes at the base of the Sangre de Cristo Mountains?

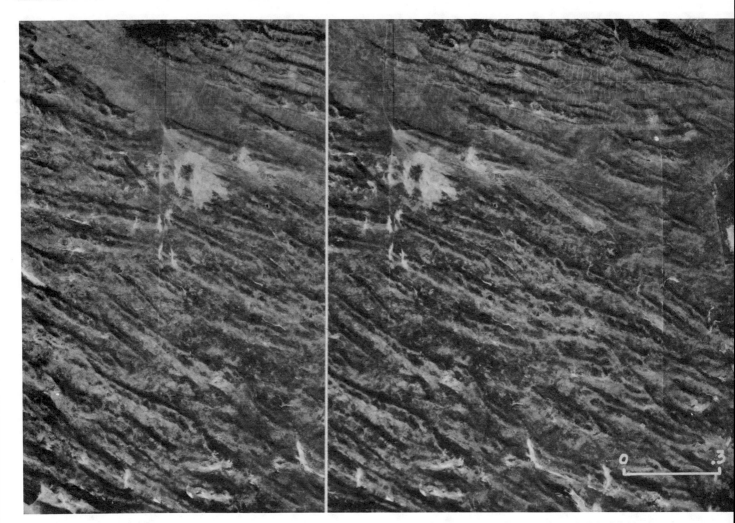

Figure 29.6. Stabilized seif, or longitudinal, dunes near Lone Valley, Nebraska (1:20,000) (USGS)

    b. What evidence is there for the assertion that water is helping to slow down the advance of the dunes into the area at the base of the mountains?

5. The availability of sand is a critical factor in the formation of dunes. List three different sources of sand for dune growth:

    a. _____

    b. _____

    c. _____

6. What evidence is there in Figure 29.4 that bushes, trees, or rocks are acting as obstructions to sand flow and forming obstacle dunes?

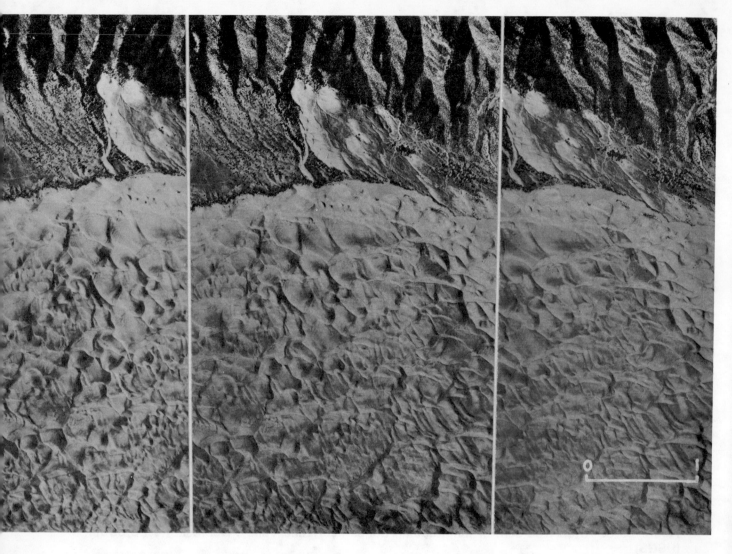

Figure 29.7. A portion of Great Sand Dunes National Park flanking the Sangre de Cristo Mountains on the east side of the San Luis Valley in Colorado (1:53,000) (USGS)

Name: _____

Laboratory section: _____

EXERCISE **30**

Coastal Landforms

The problems selected for study in this exercise show how coastlines are the result of the dynamic processes of marine erosion and deposition. Review in your textbook the following topics, which are essential background reading for these problems:

Wave erosion
Longshore (beach) drifting
Wave refraction
Sand-spit formation
Cliff formation

SHORELINE CLASSIFICATION

The variety of forms found in coastal areas is so large that classification of shoreline forms is a most useful aid to their understanding. The scheme outlined here is named after the man who developed it, F. P. Shepherd.

Shepherd's classification of coasts.

1. Primary coasts
    a. Land-erosion coasts
        Ria coast
        Drowned glacial-erosion coats
        Drowned karst topography
    b. Subaerial deposition coasts
        River-deposition coasts
        Glacial-deposition coasts
        Wind-deposition coasts
        Landslide coasts
    c. Volcanic coasts
        Lava-flow coasts
        Tephra coasts (volcanic
            fragments)
        Volcanic-collapse or -explosion
            coasts
    d. Coasts shaped by diastrophic
        movement
        Fault coasts
        Fold coasts
        Sedimentary extrusions (salt
            domes, mud lumps)

2. Secondary coasts
    a. Wave-erosion coasts
        Wave-straightened coasts
        Coasts made irregular by wave
            erosion
    b. Marine-deposition coasts
        Barrier coasts
        Cuspate forelands
        Beach plains
        Mud flats or salt marshes
    c. Coasts built by organisms
        Coral-reef coasts
        Oyster-reef coasts
        Mangrove coasts
        Marsh-grass coasts

PROBLEMS

1. The intricate relationship between erosion and sediment deposition in a marine environment is illustrated by Figure 30.1.

    a. What is the name given to this relatively flat-lying surface (see a on the photograph)? _____ How was it formed?

Figure 30.1.   The Oregon coast south of Waldport (Oregon State Highway Department)

b. There are several places where the feature identified in Problem 1a has been deeply eroded (see b on the photograph). What is your explanation for this differential erosion?

c. What evidence is there to support the assertion that the dominant winds are westerly along this coast? (Hint: Check the vegetation.)

2. Using Shepherd's coastal classification, how would you classify Figure 30.1 in one of his seven major categories? Support your decision with evidence.

Figure 30.2. Netarts Spit, Oregon (Oregon State Highway Department)

3. Bays and estuaries along this part of the Oregon coast (Figure 30.2) are partially closed by sand deposition. What do the spits and sand accumulation tell us about the availability of sediment along the coast?

4. a. What is responsible for the stabilization of the sand forming Netarts Spit (Figure 30.2)?

   b. There are places on the spit where sand movement is active and the vegetation is being overwhelmed by the sand. Put an X on the photograph marking two places of sand advance.

   c. What prevents Netarts Spit from completely sealing off Netarts Bay?

   d. How can you locate the deep-water sections of the bay?

5. In Figure 30.3 there is evidence of several marine terraces (ancient wave-cut platforms). Using a colored pencil, identify the terraces: 1 for the lowest terrace, 2 for the next highest, and so on.

6. The steep slopes separating the terraces were _____ when the sea covered the wave-cut platforms.

7. Mark an arrow (with *WR* printed beside it), to indicate an area on the stereo pair where wave refraction is evident.

.5 km

0

Figure 30.3.   Palos Verdes Hills, Los Angeles, California (USGS)

Name: _____

Laboratory section: _____

The Frequency of Occurrence of Natural Events

One of the goals of the environmental sciences is to be able to make accurate predictions for natural events such as floods (Figure 32.1), tornadoes, and extremely large rainfalls. However, the present level of understanding of these phenomena precludes precise prediction. It is simply not possible at this time to assert that a 6-in. rainfall will occur at a certain time and place.

The classical approach in science is to link every effect with its cause. This approach necessitates a thorough understanding of the processes at work, but for many, if not most, of the problems we encounter in geography this precise, deterministic approach cannot be used. The approach cannot be used because we have an inadequate understanding of the variables in a given problem and the interactions between them. Instead, physical geographers use probabilistic methods, such as the *recurrence interval*, for the analysis of natural events.

THE RECURRENCE INTERVAL

The *recurrence interval* (also called the return period) is the average interval of time within which a given flood will be equaled or exceeded once.

A flood having a recurrence interval of 10 yr is one that has a 10% chance of recurring in any year, while a 100-yr flood (or 100-yr recurrence interval) has a 1% chance of recurring.

Table 32.1 is a listing of the highest flows that occurred on the Kyte River at Flagg Center, Illinois, for each year in the time period 1940–1950. A list of these annual, extreme flows is called the *annual series*.

Steps for calculating the recurrence interval for the data in Table 32.1 are as follows:

1. Rank the floods, giving the rank of 1 to the largest flood, and enter the results into column 3 of Table 32.1.
2. Calculate the recurrence interval for each flood, using the following formula:

$$T = \frac{n + 1}{m}$$

where

T = recurrence interval (in years)
n = number of years of record
m = rank of the flood

Enter the results in Table 32.1 under column 4.

3. Plot the T value and its associated discharge on the graph paper in Figure 32.2.
4. Fit a straight line through the data points on the graph.

Figure 32.1. The flood of 12 March 1963 on the North Fork of the Kentucky River at Hazard, Kentucky. The recurrence interval of this flood was approximately 25 yr. (From Louisville *Courier-Journal* 13 March 1963, p. 1)

PROBLEMS

Answer the following questions, using the completed graph:

1. In 1951 the peak flow of the river was found to be 2000 cfs. What is the recurrence interval of that flow? _____

2. What is the discharge for a recurrence interval of 20 yr?

Table 32.1. Kyte River Near Flagg Center, Illinois

1	2	3	4
Time of Flood	Discharge (cfs)	Rank	Recurrence Interval
4 Mar. 1940	800	———	———
13 Feb. 1941	1080	———	———
2 Aug. 1942	692	———	———
16 Mar. 1943	1380	———	———
15 Mar. 1944	1280	———	———
17 May 1945	889	———	———
6 Jan. 1946	2030	———	———
5 Apr. 1947	890	———	———
20 Mar. 1948	1480	———	———
19 Feb. 1949	1600	———	———
6 Mar. 1950	1330	———	———

Drainage Basin Area: 125 mi^2

3. Explain what is meant by the statement "A discharge of 2030 cfs on the Kyte River has a recurrence interval of 12 yr." In other words, explain to the person uninitiated to ideas about return periods what is meant by the statement.

4. Given the information in Figure 32.1, how many times in 100 yr would you expect this size flood to occur?

5. What is the danger in extrapolating the data in Figure 32.2 beyond a recurrence interval of 12 yr?

EXTREME RAINFALLS

Most people have a fascination for climatic gee-whiz statistics of the following sort:

Most rainfall in 12 mo: *1042 in.*, Cherrapunji, India, August 1860–July 1861.

Greatest average annual precipitation in the conterminous United States: *144 in.*, Wynoorhee, Washington.

Most rainfall in 1 min: *1.23 in.*, Unionville, Maryland, 4 July 1956.

These pieces of information give a dramatic view of the range of climatic conditions that can be expected. Not so spectacular are the extreme rainfalls of different durations which have been mapped for the United States and Canada in the following publications:

Bruce, J. P. 1968. *Atlas of rainfall intensity-duration frequency data for Canada.* Toronto: Department of Transport, Meteorological Branch Climatological Studies No. 8.

Hershfield, D. M. 1961. *Rainfall frequency atlas of the United States.* U.S. Weather Bureau Technical Paper No. 40.

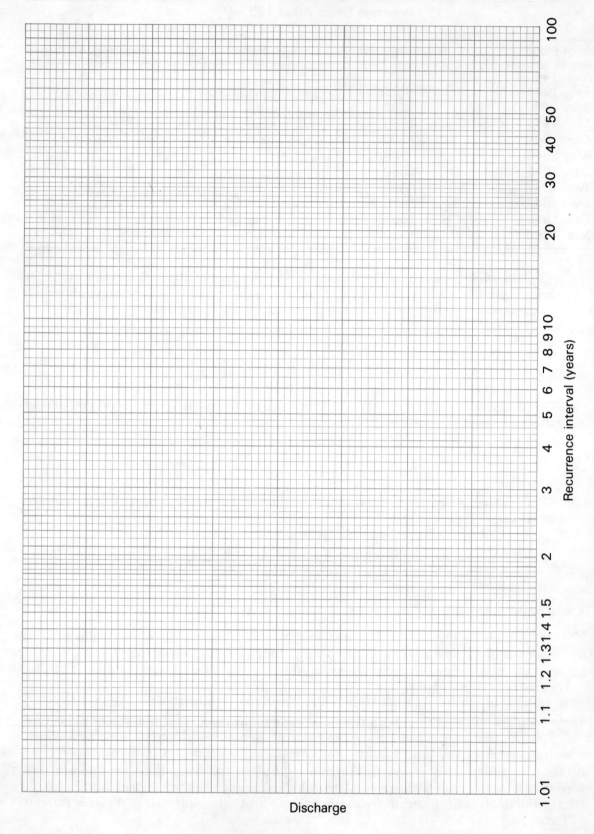

Figure 32.2. Graph paper for plotting recurrence interval and associated discharge

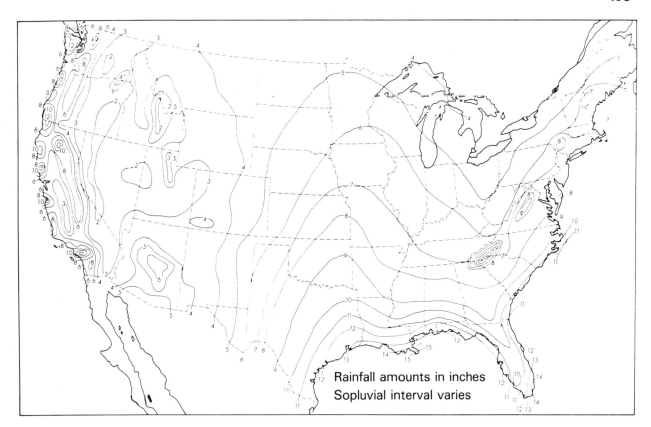

Figure 32.3. Map showing 24-hr rainfall (in.) with 100-yr recurrence interval (U.S. Department of Commerce, Weather Bureau Technical Paper No. 40)

These atlases have maps that show rainfalls of different durations (30 min, 1 hr, 2 hr, 3 hr, 24 hr, and so on) and different return periods. The great value of these maps is that they provide the user with an immediate value for a rainfall at a given location.

PROBLEMS

An example of one of these maps is given in Figure 32.3. Answer the following questions.

6. In which state, Florida or Minnesota, must the greatest care be taken in estimating precipitation for a dam site? _____

7. Suggest an explanation for the very heavy rainfalls that occur along the Gulf coast.

8. From the isohyets, estimate the expected 100 yr, 24 hr rainfall for your college's location. _____

9. The study of the impact of extreme geophysical events on human populations is called natural-hazard research. List two natural hazards that have occurred in the last year in the vicinity of your college.

   a.

   b.

10. Droughts result in low streamflow. List three environmental impacts that come about because of unusually low flows and tell why you think they are a result of drought.

Name: _____

Laboratory section: _____

A Case Study of an Environmental Hazard—Land Subsidence in Long Beach, California

The subsidence of land is an environmental hazard caused by both human actions and natural processes; it varies in intensity from sudden drops in land elevation to movements so imperceptible that they can be sensed only by instruments. The effects of these ground-level changes on human activities can be severe and includes:

Flooding
Collapse of, or structural damage to, buildings
Buckling of roads and railroads
The shearing off of water and oil wells

This exercise examines the impact of oil-field development on Long Beach, California (Figure 33.1). Read over the whole exercise before you answer any of the questions.

DEVELOPMENT OF THE OIL FIELD

Long Beach straddles part of a faulted, asymmetrical anticline that is the structure responsible for the oil reservoir forming the Wilmington Oil Field (Figure 33.2). Within 6 yr of the field's discovery in 1936, there were nearly 1000 producing wells; within the city limits the spacing of wells was so close that the density reached one well per 2.3 acres.

PROBLEMS

1. Plot the data in Table 33.1 on the graph paper (Figure 33.3). Put oil production on the vertical axis and time (years) along the horizontal axis; use as much of the axes as possible. Connect the data with straight lines; use a colored pencil.

LAND SUBSIDENCE

Land subsidence became evident as the oil field was intensely developed in the early 1940s (Table 33.2). Whereas at one time the land was above high-tide level, with subsidence parts of Terminal Island (Figure 33.1) were being inundated during high water. As the subsidence became more pronounced, diking and land-filling became necessary in conjunction with the structural raising of wharves and warehouses.

PROBLEMS

2. Using the graph (Figure 33.3) on which you have previously plotted oil production, insert the data from Table 33.2. You will find it advantageous to have a vertical scale such that the highest value will be below the oil-production line.
    Use a colored pencil different from that used for joining the points.

Figure 33.1. Subsidence of the Wilmington Oil Field at Long Beach, California. Subsidence contours in ft. (Long Beach Department of Oil Properties)

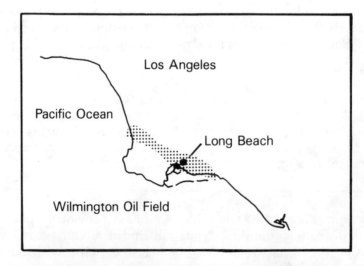

Figure 33.2. The Wilmington Oil Field, California

**Table 33.1. Oil Production in the Wilmington Oil Field: 1937–1968
(thousands of barrels/day)**

1937	0	1945	99	1953	127	1961	76
1938	100	1946	93	1954	117	1962	82
1939	80	1947	117	1955	110	1963	90
1940	85	1948	136	1956	105	1964	97
1941	80	1949	127	1957	100	1965	97
1942	87	1950	110	1958	85	1966	102
1943	94	1951	142	1959	80	1967	150
1944	98	1952	133	1960	75	1968	167

WATER INJECTION

The severity of the land subsidence problem required action, and in 1958 the city decided that the solution to the environmental problems lay with the restoration of pressure in the oil field. Consequently, a water-injection program was established with an injection rate of 750,000 barrels of salt water per day. Subsidence rates halted, and a few places even began rebounding.

PROBLEMS

3. You will now plot a third relationship on the graph: the information in Table 33.3. Use the same horizontal-axis scale (years) as in the previous questions. Join the points with a third colored pencil.

4. a. From 1947 until 1959 the oil production rate and the rate of subsidence moved in tandem. Suggest an explanation for this.

   b. From 1959 onward, even though oil production increased, the rate of subsidence continued to fall. Explain.

5. Suggest another type of land subsidence (other than in oil fields) where water injection might work to slow down or halt subsidence.

Years

Figure 33.3.   Graph paper for plotting data from Table 33.1

Table 33.2. Subsidence Rate: 1947–1968
(in./yr)

1947	13.0	1953	24.0	1959	12.5	1965	2.5
1948	17.0	1954	20.0	1960	10.0	1966	3.0
1949	21.0	1955	17.5	1961	7.5	1967	0.5
1950	21.5	1956	18.3	1962	8.5	1968	0.5
1951	22.0	1957	15.0	1963	4.5		
1952	29.0	1958	14.0	1964	3.5		

Table 33.3. Water Injection: 1958–1968
(thousands of barrels/day)

1958	35	1964	520
1959	160	1965	560
1960	250	1966	520
1961	290	1967	720
1962	360	1968	820
1963	440		

6. If you were the environmental manager of an area where oil was found close to the surface in relatively soft rocks, what measures would you undertake to monitor the possibility of land subsidence?

7. Draw the profile X–Y from Figure 33.1, assuming a scale of 1 cm = 2000 m. Plot subsidence on the vertical scale and distance on the horizontal.

EXERCISE **34**
The Tides

Tides are a major factor to life along coastlines. The tides, which normally ebb and flow twice a day, are caused by several forces: the gravitational attraction of the moon, the gravitational attraction of the sun, and the centrifugal forces as the earth-moon system revolves about the sun. The moon is far more important than the sun in determining the tides. The strength of the sun on the tides is such that it only modifies the lunar tide. The tides, although averaging twice a day, vary considerably with time and from place to place, but always in a predictable manner at a given location. This allows the tides to be predicted well in advance.

PROBLEMS

1. Using the data given in Table 34.1 complete Table 34.2.
2. What is the average time interval between high and low tides on October 14?

   _____

3. Explain why on some calendar days there is only one high tide or one low tide indicated.

4. What is the mean tidal range (difference between high and low tide) for 14 and 15 October? _____
5. What is the mean tidal range for 21 and 22 October? _____
6. What is the time interval between high and low tides at Boston?

   _____

7. What is the earliest date following 22 October that the range again reaches or exceeds 13 ft? _____
8. What is the time interval between the date of the highest tidal range in October and the highest tidal range in November? _____
9. Why are these spring tides higher than those of the weeks in-between?

Table 34.1 Times and Heights of High and Low Waters for Boston, Massachusetts, in 1981

October

Day	Time	ft	m	Day	Time	ft	m
1 Th	0051	9.6	2.9	16 F	0042	10.9	3.3
	0655	0.2	0.1		0648	-1.2	-0.4
	1307	9.8	3.0		1300	11.7	3.6
	1919	-0.1	0.0		1921	-2.0	-0.6
2 F	0132	9.2	2.8	17 Sa	0135	10.5	3.2
	0735	0.6	0.2		0738	-0.8	-0.2
	1346	9.6	2.9		1353	11.4	3.5
	2001	0.2	0.1		2013	-1.6	-0.5
3 Sa	0215	8.9	2.7	18 Su	0230	10.1	3.1
	0817	0.9	0.3		0832	-0.3	-0.1
	1428	9.3	2.8		1448	11.0	3.4
	2046	0.5	0.2		2110	-1.1	-0.3
4 Su	0259	8.5	2.6	19 M	0329	9.6	2.9
	0902	1.3	0.4		0931	0.2	0.1
	1515	9.0	2.7		1547	10.5	3.2
	2134	0.8	0.2		2211	-0.6	-0.2
5 M	0347	8.2	2.5	20 Tu	0430	9.2	2.8
	0951	1.6	0.5		1034	0.6	0.2
	1605	8.8	2.7		1652	10.0	3.0
	2227	1.0	0.3		2316	-0.2	-0.1
6 Tu	0440	8.0	2.4	21 W	0536	9.0	2.7
	1044	1.8	0.5		1139	0.8	0.2
	1658	8.7	2.7		1758	9.7	3.0
	2322	1.1	0.3				
7 W	0536	7.9	2.4	22 Th	0021	0.0	0.0
	1140	1.8	0.5		0642	9.0	2.7
	1753	8.8	2.7		1248	0.8	0.2
					1903	9.6	2.9
8 Th	0020	0.9	0.3	23 F	0125	0.0	0.0
	0632	8.1	2.5		0744	9.2	2.8
	1239	1.5	0.5		1349	0.6	0.2
	1848	9.0	2.7		2003	9.6	2.9
9 F	0114	0.6	0.2	24 Sa	0219	0.0	0.0
	0725	8.6	2.6		0839	9.4	2.9
	1334	1.0	0.3		1444	0.3	0.1
	1944	9.4	2.9		2058	9.6	2.9
10 Sa	0205	0.2	0.1	25 Su	0307	0.0	0.0
	0816	9.1	2.8		0924	9.7	3.0
	1426	0.4	0.1		1531	0.0	0.0
	2035	9.9	3.0		2145	9.6	2.9
11 Su	0253	-0.3	-0.1	26 M	0349	-0.1	0.0
	0904	9.8	3.0		1007	9.9	3.0
	1514	-0.3	-0.1		1615	-0.2	-0.1
	2125	10.4	3.2		2229	9.6	2.9
12 M	0340	-0.8	-0.2	27 Tu	0431	0.0	0.0
	0949	10.5	3.2		1044	10.0	3.0
	1604	-1.0	-0.3		1654	-0.4	-0.1
	2213	10.8	3.3		2308	9.5	2.9
13 Tu	0425	-1.2	-0.4	28 W	0507	0.1	0.0
	1036	11.1	3.4		1121	10.0	3.0
	1651	-1.6	-0.5		1733	-0.4	-0.1
	2302	11.0	3.4		2347	9.4	2.9
14 W	0511	-1.4	-0.4	29 Th	0546	0.3	0.1
	1124	11.5	3.5		1158	10.0	3.0
	1740	-2.0	-0.6		1812	-0.4	-0.1
	2351	11.0	3.4				
15 Th	0559	-1.4	-0.4	30 F	0026	9.2	2.8
	1211	11.7	3.6		0624	0.5	0.2
	1829	-2.1	-0.6		1235	9.8	3.0
					1851	-0.2	-0.1
				31 Sa	0103	9.0	2.7
					0703	0.7	0.2
					1314	9.6	2.9
					1932	0.0	0.0

November

Day	Time	ft	m	Day	Time	ft	m
1 Su	0145	8.7	2.7	16 M	0214	10.0	3.0
	0745	1.0	0.3		0813	-0.4	-0.1
	1356	9.4	2.9		1430	11.0	3.4
	2015	0.2	0.1		2052	-1.3	-0.4
2 M	0230	8.4	2.6	17 Tu	0312	9.6	2.9
	0828	1.3	0.4		0912	0.1	0.0
	1441	9.1	2.8		1529	10.4	3.2
	2102	0.5	0.2		2152	-0.7	-0.2
3 Tu	0318	8.2	2.5	18 W	0414	9.3	2.8
	0918	1.6	0.5		1014	0.6	0.2
	1528	8.9	2.7		1630	9.9	3.0
	2152	0.7	0.2		2255	-0.3	-0.1
4 W	0406	8.1	2.5	19 Th	0516	9.1	2.8
	1009	1.7	0.5		1119	0.8	0.2
	1620	8.8	2.7		1736	9.4	2.9
	2246	0.7	0.2		2356	0.1	0.0
5 Th	0459	8.2	2.5	20 F	0619	9.1	2.8
	1104	1.6	0.5		1224	0.8	0.2
	1715	8.8	2.7		1838	9.1	2.8
	2341	0.7	0.2				
6 F	0555	8.4	2.6	21 Sa	0055	0.3	0.1
	1202	1.3	0.4		0715	9.2	2.8
	1813	9.0	2.7		1324	0.6	0.2
					1942	9.0	2.7
7 Sa	0035	0.4	0.1	22 Su	0149	0.3	0.1
	0648	8.9	2.7		0809	9.4	2.9
	1300	0.8	0.2		1419	0.4	0.1
	1909	9.3	2.8		2033	9.0	2.7
8 Su	0128	0.0	0.0	23 M	0238	0.4	0.1
	0741	9.5	2.9		0855	9.6	2.9
	1355	0.1	0.0		1506	0.1	0.0
	2004	9.8	3.0		2122	9.0	2.7
9 M	0219	-0.4	-0.1	24 Tu	0319	0.4	0.1
	0832	10.3	3.1		0938	9.7	3.0
	1447	-0.7	-0.2		1551	-0.1	0.0
	2055	10.2	3.1		2204	9.0	2.7
10 Tu	0309	-0.9	-0.3	25 W	0401	0.4	0.1
	0919	11.0	3.4		1015	9.8	3.0
	1538	-1.4	-0.4		1631	-0.3	-0.1
	2148	10.5	3.2		2243	9.0	2.7
11 W	0357	-1.2	-0.4	26 Th	0441	0.4	0.1
	1009	11.5	3.5		1052	9.9	3.0
	1629	-2.0	-0.6		1710	-0.4	-0.1
	2239	10.8	3.3		2323	8.9	2.7
12 Th	0446	-1.4	-0.4	27 F	0518	0.5	0.2
	1058	11.9	3.6		1131	9.9	3.0
	1719	-2.4	-0.7		1748	-0.4	-0.1
	2332	10.8	3.3				
13 F	0535	-1.4	-0.4	28 Sa	0000	8.9	2.7
	1149	12.1	3.7		0557	0.6	0.2
	1810	-2.5	-0.8		1208	9.8	3.0
					1827	-0.4	-0.1
14 Sa	0023	10.7	3.3	29 Su	0039	8.8	2.7
	0625	-1.2	-0.4		0637	0.7	0.2
	1240	11.9	3.6		1246	9.7	3.0
	1902	-2.3	-0.7		1907	-0.3	-0.1
15 Su	0118	10.4	3.2	30 M	0120	8.6	2.6
	0718	-0.8	-0.2		0717	0.9	0.3
	1334	11.6	3.5		1329	9.5	2.9
	1956	-1.9	-0.6		1948	-0.1	0.0

December

Day	Time	ft	m	Day	Time	ft	m
1 Tu	0203	8.5	2.6	16 W	0251	9.7	3.0
	0801	1.1	0.3		0849	0.0	0.0
	1411	9.4	2.9		1507	10.3	3.1
	2034	0.1	0.0		2126	-0.8	-0.2
2 W	0248	8.4	2.6	17 Th	0349	9.4	2.9
	0848	1.2	0.4		0949	0.4	0.1
	1457	9.2	2.8		1606	9.7	3.0
	2121	0.2	0.1		2224	-0.3	-0.1
3 Th	0334	8.4	2.6	18 F	0445	9.1	2.8
	0937	1.3	0.4		1051	0.7	0.2
	1545	9.1	2.8		1705	9.1	2.8
	2211	0.3	0.1		2321	0.2	0.1
4 F	0427	8.5	2.6	19 Sa	0544	9.0	2.7
	1032	1.2	0.4		1153	0.8	0.2
	1643	9.0	2.7		1806	8.7	2.7
	2303	0.3	0.1				
5 Sa	0519	8.8	2.7	20 Su	0017	0.5	0.2
	1130	0.9	0.3		0639	9.0	2.7
	1739	9.1	2.8		1254	0.8	0.2
	2358	0.1	0.0		1903	8.4	2.6
6 Su	0612	9.3	2.8	21 M	0112	0.7	0.2
	1228	0.4	0.1		0731	9.1	2.8
	1836	9.2	2.8		1349	0.6	0.2
					1959	8.3	2.5
7 M	0053	-0.1	0.0	22 Tu	0202	0.8	0.2
	0707	9.9	3.0		0820	9.3	2.8
	1326	-0.2	-0.1		1439	0.4	0.1
	1933	9.5	2.9		2050	8.3	2.5
8 Tu	0146	-0.4	-0.1	23 W	0248	0.8	0.2
	0800	10.5	3.2		0904	9.4	2.9
	1422	-0.9	-0.3		1522	0.1	0.0
	2031	9.8	3.0		2135	8.4	2.6
9 W	0240	-0.8	-0.2	24 Th	0330	0.7	0.2
	0853	11.1	3.4		0945	9.6	2.9
	1516	-1.6	-0.5		1604	-0.1	0.0
	2126	10.1	3.1		2217	8.5	2.6
10 Th	0332	-1.0	-0.3	25 F	0412	0.7	0.2
	0945	11.6	3.5		1025	9.7	3.0
	1609	-2.1	-0.6		1645	-0.3	-0.1
	2220	10.3	3.1		2257	8.6	2.6
11 F	0423	-1.2	-0.4	26 Sa	0452	0.6	0.2
	1037	12.0	3.7		1105	9.8	3.0
	1702	-2.4	-0.7		1724	-0.4	-0.1
	2313	10.4	3.2		2336	8.6	2.6
12 Sa	0515	-1.3	-0.4	27 Su	0533	0.6	0.2
	1130	12.1	3.7		1143	9.8	3.0
	1753	-2.5	-0.8		1805	-0.5	-0.2
13 Su	0007	10.4	3.2	28 M	0015	8.7	2.7
	0607	-1.2	-0.4		0612	0.6	0.2
	1223	11.9	3.6		1223	9.8	3.0
	1845	-2.3	-0.7		1844	-0.5	-0.2
14 M	0101	10.2	3.1	29 Tu	0056	8.7	2.7
	0700	-0.9	-0.3		0653	0.6	0.2
	1316	11.5	3.5		1304	9.8	3.0
	1938	-1.9	-0.6		1924	-0.5	-0.2
15 Tu	0155	10.0	3.0	30 W	0137	8.8	2.7
	0753	-0.5	-0.2		0737	0.6	0.2
	1411	11.0	3.4		1346	9.7	3.0
	2032	-1.4	-0.4		2006	-0.4	-0.1
				31 Th	0220	8.8	2.7
					0823	0.6	0.2
					1432	9.5	2.9
					2052	-0.3	-0.1

Time meridian 75 degrees west. 0000 is midnight. 1200 is noon. Heights are referenced to mean low water.

Source: U.S. Department of Commerce. NOAA. Tide Tables, 1981. East coast of North America and South America, including Greenland.

Table 34.2. Time and Height of Tides in Boston Harbor

	Time	Height	Time	Height	Time	Height	Time	Height
			14 October				**15–16 October**	
High	11:24	11.5	___	___	___	___	___	___
Low	05:11	−1.4	___	___	___	___	___	___
Difference	6:13	12.9	___	___	___	___	___	___
			21 October				**22–23 October**	
High	___	___	___	___	___	___	___	___
Low	___	___	___	___	___	___	___	___
Difference	___	___	___	___	___	___	___	___

10. On what date in December would you expect the spring tide to reach a maximum? _____

11. What is the maximum range on that date? _____

12. The range in the tide varies with location, largely because of the topography of the coastline. The range in tides is the lowest over the open ocean. Using the data in Table 34.3, determine the mean range of the spring tides at Chappaquiddick Island and Nantucket Island. _____

13. What is the ratio of the range of the spring tide in Boston Harbor to that of Nantucket Island and Chappaquiddick Island? _____

14. Using a map of the Bay of Fundy area, explain the 43.6-ft range in the spring tides at Horton Bluff, Nova Scotia.

Table 34.3. Tidal Range and Mean Tidal Height for Selected Locations

Place	Tidal Range (ft) Mean	Spring	Mean Level of High Tide
Wasque Point, Chappaquiddick Island	1.1	1.4	0.6
Tom Nevers Head, Nantucket Island	1.2	1.4	0.6
New York City, the Battery	4.5	5.4	2.2
New York City, Coney Island	4.7	5.7	2.3
Boston Harbor	9.5	11.0	4.7
Steele Harbor Island, Maine	11.6	13.3	5.8
Eastport, Maine	18.2	20.7	9.1
Saint John, New Brunswick, Bay of Fundy, Nova Scotia	20.8	23.7	14.4
Spicer Cove, Chignecto Bay, Bay of Fundy, Nova Scotia	27.0	30.0	18.3
Spencers Island, Bay of Fundy, Nova Scotia	30.5	35.0	21.2
Horton Bluff, Avon River, Bay of Fundy, Nova Scotia	38.1	43.6	24.6

Spatial Distribution and Controls on Individual Plant Species

This exercise and the one that follows are designed to show both the complexities and the regularities inherent in the geography of plants. Rather than starting off with the involved interactions of the ecosystem, these exercises will concentrate on the individual plant species.

SPECIES

"Although each plant is in some way morphologically unique, careful examination of a large number of plants reveals that these tend to fall into a number of fairly distinct categories on the basis of external appearance" (M.C. Kellman, 1980, *Plant geography*, 2nd ed., London: Methuen, p. 6). These categories based on morphological and physiological characteristics are called *species*. A species is a group of cross-pollinating individuals existing in similar environment.

THE SPECIES AND THE ENVIRONMENT

The individual plant reflects the adaption of a given species to its environment. For a plant to thrive, it must have a sufficient supply of nutrients and tolerable environmental conditions. The physical factors influencing plant growth include the following major ones:

Temperature	Solar radiation
Soil moisture	Atmospheric gases
Fire	Soil
Humidity	Wind

In evaluating these factors, note that plants *adapt* to the environment and *modify* it. Further, interaction with other plants can help a plant adapt to its surroundings.

THE RANGE OF A PLANT SPECIES

Given the limiting influence of nutrient and environmental factors, a plant will occur over a limited area. This region or spatial distribution is called the *range* of a species. Conceptually, the range of a plant has two aspects: *potential range* and *actual range*. The potential range of a plant is the area that a plant, given its physiological properties, should be able to grow in. However, the actual range of a plant is much less than its potential because of such constraints as the limited ability of the plant to migrate from its source area to all parts of the range. At the extremities of the range, the plant is exposed to greater variance in environmental conditions. Complicating the picture even further is the fact that a species adapts differently in different parts of the range. For example, the Douglas fir growing in central California is far more susceptible to frost (in its early years of growth) than the Douglas fir of central British Columbia.

PROBLEMS

Eastern Hemlock (*Tsuga canadensis*).   Eastern hemlock is found in areas with humid, cool climates, though at the limits of the range, average annual precipitation is as low as 28 in. (711 mm). In the western and southern parts of the range, topography is a crucial factor, for hemlock is restricted to cool valleys and north-facing slopes.

1. What was the migration rate (meters per year) of hemlock between the locations X and Y in Figure 35.1? _____
2. In what part of the range is hemlock expanding? _____
3. Where is the range contracting? _____
4. Examine the lines of hemlock migration and then answer the following questions:
   a. Did the eastern hemlock migrate more rapidly between 1000 and 2000 yr ago or between 9000 and 10,000 yr ago? _____

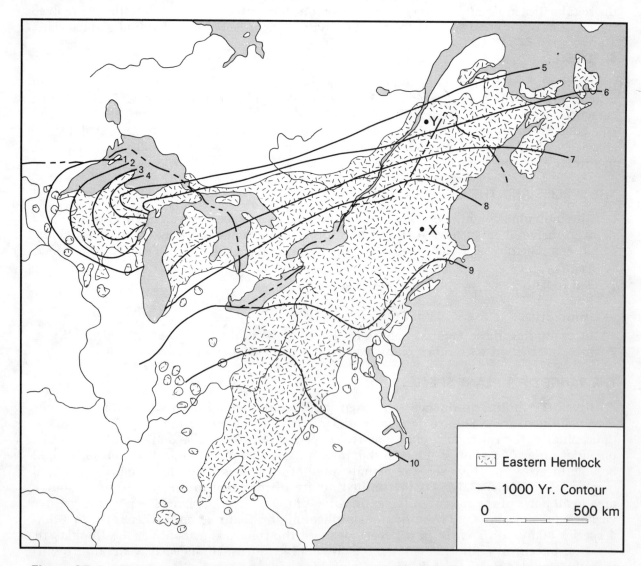

Figure 35.1.   The present range of eastern hemlock and its migration route since the end of the last glaciation. Isochrons represent thousands of years before present. (Isochrons are derived from M. B. Davis, 1976, *Geoscience and man,* 13: 13-26)

b. The northern migration of eastern hemlock followed the retreat of

_____ .

c. Place on Figure 35.1 a line marking the southern boundary of the Wisconsinan ice at its maximum extent.

5. Suggest an explanation for the peninsula-shaped extension of eastern hemlock into the southeastern states.

Pollen Diagram Interpretation

6. What were the dominant species in the area of this lake (Figure 35.2) up until 6000 yr B.P. (before present)?

7. a. Spruce has a bimodal frequency distribution. Explain.

b. Has spruce been declining or increasing in importance since 4000 yr B.P.?

8. Describe how Figure 35.2 shows the changing nature of the natural vegetation around this lake over a 14,000-yr time span.

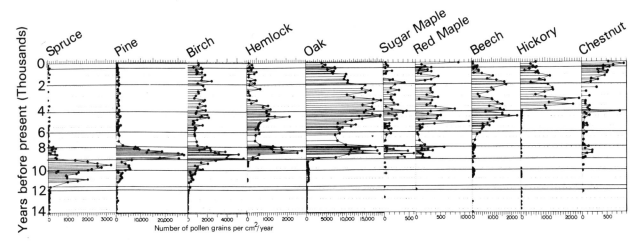

Figure 35.2. Accumulation of pollen in Rogers Lake, Connecticut (After M. B. Davis et al., 1973, *Quaternary plant ecology*. London: Blackwell)

9. Using your textbook, compare and contrast the maps of climate and natural vegetation. With that general information in mind, examine Figure 35.2 and write a paragraph on the climatic implications of this data.

Geographical Scale and the Plant Species

10. a. Which levels of the hierarchy (Figure 35.3) represent continuous distributions?

    b. Which levels of the hierarchy represent point distributions?

    c. At which level can you associate the occurrence of *Tetraphis* with a distinctive feature rather than just a point in space?

11. The levels of the range for *Tetraphis* (Figure 35.3) are governed by different environmental limiting factors. Insert the correct hierarchy level [*continent, cluster,* or *locality*] beside each limiting factor.

Limiting Factors	Hierarchy Level
Relative humidity	_____
Temperature, relative humidity, oceanic effects	_____
Shady conditions, pH variations	_____

12. Discuss three different reasons why the theoretical and actual ranges of a plant species rarely coincide.

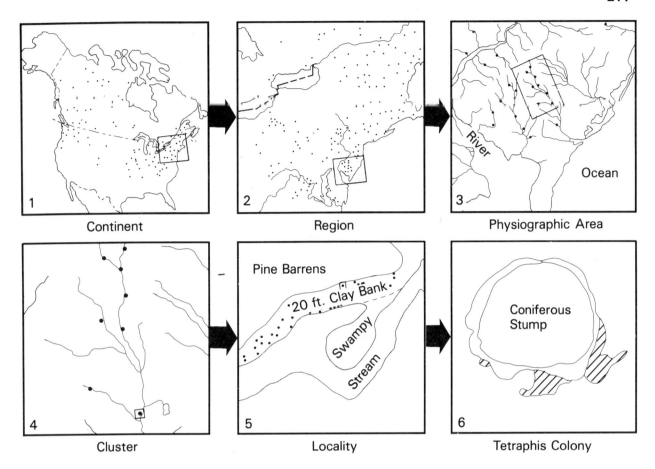

Figure 35.3. Maps of *Tetraphis* showing its spatial distribution at differing geographic scales (Adapted from R. T. T. Forman, 1964, *Ecological monographs,* 34: 1-25)

4. The map of biomes (Figure 36.1) shows a largely east-west trend in Canada but a north-south trend in the United States. How do you account for this?

5. The major grassland biome in North America (check your answers to question 3) stretches from the U.S.–Mexican border in Texas to central Saskatchewan. What are the *limiting factors* on its eastern, western, and northern boundaries?

6. The mountain chains of western North America show distinct vegetational zonation. Describe this zonation with the aid of a diagram.

7. South-central California is in the chaparral biome. A similar vegetation exists around the Mediterranean Sea. What are the reasons for the similarity between the two widely separated areas?

8. Figure 36.2B is a north-south transect across North America.
   a. What is the major climatic factor influencing this vegetational transect?

   b. Identify an ecotone. Clearly mark your answer on Figure 36.2.

   c. Where is oak-hickory forest located in North America?

9. Define the following:
   a. Succession

   b. Xerophytes

Mesophytic forest   Oak-hickory forest   Oak woodland   Prairie   Dry grasslands   Desert

(A)

Tropical forest   Subtropical forest   Temperate deciduous forest   Temperate mixed forest   Boreal forest   Tundra

(B)

Figure 36.2. An east-west transect (A) and a north-south transect (B) across North America from the tundra in northern Canada to the tropical forests of Mexico (Figure 17.3, p. 538, in *Ecology and field biology*, 2nd ed., by Robert Leo Smith. Copyright 1966, 1974 by Robert Leo Smith. By permission of Harper and Row, publishers)

    c. Tundra

    d. Zonal soils

10.   Compare and contrast the vegetational base of the forest industry in western Canada and the Pacific Northwest with that of the southeastern states of the United States.

11.   The transect in Figure 36.2A is largely a function of precipitation. Explain.

EXERCISE *37*

Soil—A Review

One of the most critical parts of the physical landscape, at least as far as humans are concerned, is soil. This is the material that forms the outer "rind" of most of the world's land surfaces. Its relevance to us is evident in that this is the medium that ultimately determines much of our supply of food, shelter, and fiber. For the geographer who is interested in land-human relationships, knowledge of the soil is a must.

This exercise is designed to review the major properties of soil.

DEFINITION

For some people definitions hide more than they reveal, so we offer two definitions:

Soil is the collection of natural bodies occupying portions of the earth's surface that supports plants and that has properties due to the integrated effect of climate and living matter, acting upon parent material, as conditioned by relief, over periods of time. (USDA, 1951, *Soil survey manual,* Agricultural Handbook No. 18, p. 8)

Soil is what plants grow in. (G.V. Jacks, 1954, *Soil,* London: Thomas Nelson and Sons, p. 1)

SOIL PROFILES

Every soil has a profile. This is revealed by the layering effect we can observe in road cuts, trenches, or quarries when we closely examine the makeup of the earth materials from the surface down. These layers or *horizons* can be used to distinguish one soil from another. They differ in various combinations of color, texture, structure, and permeability. Most soils, but not all, have three major horizons identified by the letters A, B, and C. These horizons are often subdivided, as for example: A_{00}, A_1, B_2.

A Hypothetical Soil Profile (Figure 37.1).   The *A* horizon is that part of the soil profile containing the greatest quantity of organic matter. Water infiltrating into the soil will move through the *A* horizon removing (leaching) soluble material and clay particles. The leached material is deposited in the underlying *B* horizon. With its higher clay content, this horizon tends to be more compact and harder than either *A* or *C* horizons. Further, the *B* horizon is often intermediate in color between those above and below.

The C horizon is the decayed, broken-down rock material from which the overlying layers are formed. The frequently lighter-colored C horizon is the *parent material* of a given soil.

Simplified Soil Profiles.   Figure 37.2 illustrates four soils of worldwide extent. It is quite clear that the type and variety of horizons differ from soil to soil.

THE U.S. SOIL CLASSIFICATION SYSTEM

The material in the previous sections of this exercise reflects the terminology of the old U.S. soil classification. This terminology is retained here because it still is widely used. It

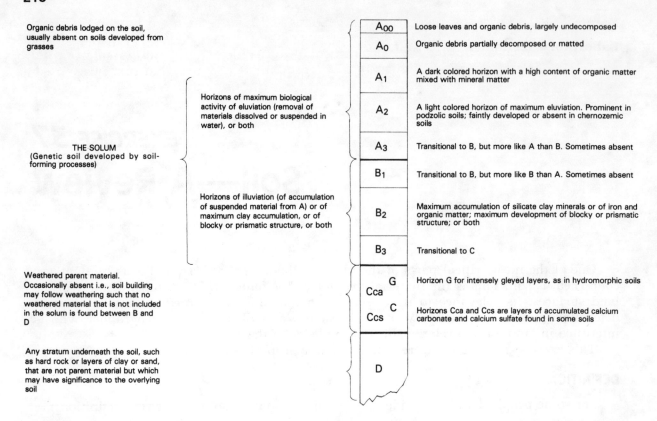

Organic debris lodged on the soil, usually absent on soils developed from grasses

A_{00} — Loose leaves and organic debris, largely undecomposed

A_0 — Organic debris partially decomposed or matted

Horizons of maximum biological activity of eluviation (removal of materials dissolved or suspended in water), or both

A_1 — A dark colored horizon with a high content of organic matter mixed with mineral matter

A_2 — A light colored horizon of maximum eluviation. Prominent in podzolic soils; faintly developed or absent in chernozemic soils

A_3 — Transitional to B, but more like A than B. Sometimes absent

THE SOLUM (Genetic soil developed by soil-forming processes)

B_1 — Transitional to B, but more like B than A. Sometimes absent

Horizons of illuviation (of accumulation of suspended material from A) or of maximum clay accumulation, or of blocky or prismatic structure, or both

B_2 — Maximum accumulation of silicate clay minerals or of iron and organic matter; maximum development of blocky or prismatic structure; or both

B_3 — Transitional to C

Weathered parent material. Occasionally absent i.e., soil building may follow weathering such that no weathered material that is not included in the solum is found between B and D

Cca G — Horizon G for intensely gleyed layers, as in hydromorphic soils

Ccs C — Horizons Cca and Ccs are layers of accumulated calcium carbonate and calcium sulfate found in some soils

Any stratum underneath the soil, such as hard rock or layers of clay or sand, that are not parent material but which may have significance to the overlying soil

D

Figure 37.1. Hypothetical soil profile having all the principal horizons (USDA, 1951, *Soil survey manual.* Agricultural Handbook No. 18, p. 175)

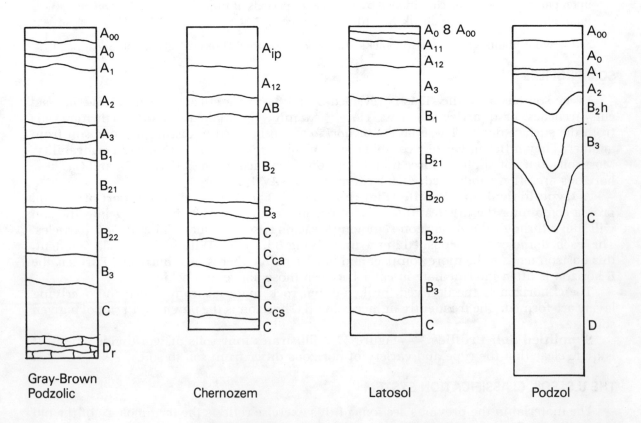

Gray-Brown Podzolic

Chernozem

Latosol

Podzol

Figure 37.2. Selected soil profiles

is found in the older soil reports, and it contains soil taxa terms used by the Food and Agriculture Organization of the United Nations and by the Canadian soil system.

The new soil classification (U.S. Department of Agriculture, Agricultural Handbook No. 436, 1975) has introduced a completely different terminology from that previously used. In this new approach emphasis is placed on the identification of two types of diagnostic soil horizons: first, the epipedon, which is formed in the upper part of the soil and contains an appreciable amount of organic matter; and second, the subsurface horizons (the names of these horizons are listed in Appendix C).

SOIL FORMATION

The formation of a soil is a complex process involving so many factors that it is extremely difficult to separate one from another. One writer has succinctly put it, "Soils are the product of their heredity and environment." Despite the difficulties of estimating their effects in an individual soil, it is possible to separate five major factors in soil formation: climate, living organisms, parent material, topography or landforms, and time.

Climate. The importance of climate to soil formation is clearly demonstrated by the way in which the world's major soil regions follow the distribution of climates. It is the interaction with temperature and precipitation that causes the breakdown of rock material. In detail, climate must be linked to leaching, the removal of solubles, and other factors.

Living organisms. The organic content of a soil is directly related to the activity of plants and animals. These, in turn, are functionally related to climate. For example, the luxuriant growth of the equatorial rainforest is a direct outcome of the high temperatures and precipitation of the equatorial climate.

Parent material. The weathering of bedrock reflects the composition of the actual rock material, so that some rocks break down rapidly and others exceedingly slowly. Some rocks, like limestone, have such distinctive characteristics that they are frequently associated with certain types of soil. Usually, however, soil is linked to its parent material but not in any clear-cut sense.

Topography (landforms). The surface of the earth is rarely completely flat. Hence, most soils are formed on sloping land. The position of a soil on a slope will greatly influence its drainage and erosion characteristics. The movement of water is rapid over and through soils on steep slopes, while there is a tendency for soils on flat areas to be badly drained. Topography, therefore, is a ubiquitous factor responsible for the minor fluctuations in soil.

Time. Soils do not form in a couple of days. Depending upon the nature of the other soil-forming properties, the time for a soil to be formed will vary. From fresh bedrock to several feet of soil is a process that requires time for weathering and time for the establishment of pioneering plant life.

SOIL PROPERTIES

When a soil is studied in the field, the observer will note certain rather obvious properties like color and texture; he will recognize that these vary from place to place. Knowledge of these characteristics will permit wise use and management of soils.

Color. This is one of the most noticeable features of a soil. A soil is rarely characterized by one color but by several, because the soil horizons usually have individual colors. In general, the colors of the upper horizons are darker than the lower horizons, for these (the upper) contain greater amounts of organic matter, which gives rise to black and brown colors. Red colors reflect unhydrated iron oxide and are typical both of well-drained locations and semiarid areas. Iron oxides also can give rise to yellow soils, though this color is often associated with higher rainfalls than the red.

Texture. The texture of a soil expresses the relative proportions of silt, sand, and clay. To express these three variables at one time, a triangular graph is used (Figures 37.3A and B). The corners of the triangle represent 100% silt, sand, and clay. The texture triangle (37.3B) is divided into units to which are applied names, which makes the comprehension of texture classes much easier.

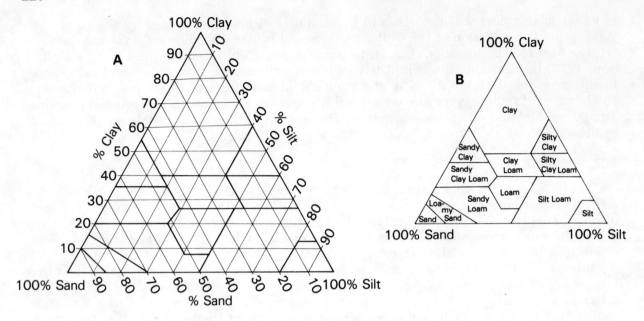

Figure 37.3. Soil texture

Example: What is the textural class of a soil with 20% clay and 70% silt? (To read the texture triangle, follow the lines in accord with the tilt of the numbers.)

Answer: Silt loam.

Structure.   This property of a soil refers to shapes taken by clusters of soil particles. A *ped* is a naturally occurring cluster or aggregate of soil particles. Peds are separated by surfaces of weakness and often have a surface film. Figure 37.4 illustrates some common types of soil structure. The usefulness of a soil with respect to crop production is largely a function of fertility and soil structure. Structure is one of the properties of soil having a direct bearing on the soil's moisture-retention capabilities. For example, where the soil peds are very loose, water will move through the soil too rapidly to be of use to the root systems of crops. Hence, these are considered droughty soils.

Air and water content.   A soil has its own atmosphere. For a soil to develop (both in terms of soil formation and plant growth), air must be held in the pore spaces. Many chemical and biological changes cannot take place without air. The volume of air in a soil is directly linked to its water content. The rate of percolation of water downward through the soil is a function of soil texture.

Organic content.   Though last in this list of soil properties, the organic content of the soil plays an important role in soil formation. When a soil is immature, it consists mainly of mineral particles derived from the parent material. Over time the organic content will increase as vegetation firmly establishes itself on the immature soil. Differences in the amount of organic matter in the vertical profile influence the degree of horizon differentiation.

PROBLEMS

1. You have discovered that a soil has:

Clay	10%
Silt	30%
Sand	60%

    Name that soil in terms of a texture class. _____

2. Suggest ways in which a soil profile may be truncated:

Kind of Structure	Description		Horizon
Crumb 	Aggregates are small, porous, and weakly held together	Nearly spherical, with many irregular surfaces	Usually found in surface soil or A horizon
Platy 	Aggregates are flat or plate-like, with horizontal dimensions greater than the vertical. Plates overlap, usually causing slow permeability		Usually found in subsurface or A₂ horizon of timber and claypan soil
Angular Blocky or Cube-Like 	Aggregates have sides at nearly right angles, tend to overlap	Nearly block-like, with 6 or more sides. All 3 dimensions about the same	
Prismatic 	Without rounded caps	Prism-like with the vertical axis greater than the horizontal	Usually found in subsoil or B horizon
Columnar 	With rounded caps		
Structure Lacking, Single Grain	Soil particles exist individually (as in sand) and do not form aggregates		Usually found in substratum or C horizon
Massive	Soil material clings together in large uniform masses (as in loess)		

Figure 37.4. Selected soil structures

3. Name the common mineral most resistant to weathering. _____

4. What effect does the addition of organic matter (humus) have on a sandy soil?

5. What kind of soil (in terms of texture) would you expect in the following environments?

   Outwash plain _____
   Floodplains _____
   On limestone _____

6. Use a world soil map for the following questions.
   a. What soil type is most typical of steppes or prairies? _____
   b. What is the typical soil of the tropics? _____
   c. Where are podzols found?

   d. What is an alluvial soil and where is it found?

7. Of soil texture and soil structure, which can be most readily modified by farming?

8. The black soils of the prairies contain calcium carbonate ($CaCO_3$), but the occurrence of this mineral in soils of more humid areas is rare. Explain why. (The exercise on limestone landforms will be helpful here.)

9. In your textbook (or atlas), compare the world maps of climate, soils, and vegetation. Then answer the following questions.
   a. What climates are associated with prairie or steppe soils?

   b. The coniferous forests that extend across the northern hemisphere correlate with which soil and climatic groups?

   c. Where are latosols (laterites) found?

   d. What is the great soil group of the area in which your college is located?

Soils and the Landscape

One of the most useful ways of summarizing soil information is in the form of a map. From the map it is possible to detect the spatial relationships between soils and the larger features of the landscape. This exercise is designed to show the relationship between soils and the landforms of a region.

SOURCES OF SOIL MAPS

Detailed soil maps of the United States are published on a county basis by the U.S. Department of Agriculture; these maps are accompanied by detailed soil descriptions and interpretations; this exercise will use the *Allen County, Indiana, soil survey report* (1969). The best way to check the availability of soil maps for a particular area is to contact the local county extension agent (USDA) or the agricultural experiment stations located at many land-grant universities. In Canada, soil maps can be obtained from the Soil Research Institute, Agriculture Canada, Ottawa, Ontario, Canada K1A 0C6.

THE GENERAL SOIL MAP

A USDA soil survey of a county will contain both a generalized map (see Figure 38.1) and a set of detailed maps. These later maps show the distribution of a *soil series*, which is a group of soils having similar soil horizons. To facilitate the mapping of soil series, it is usually subdivided into *soil types*.

For example, within a series, all the soils having a surface layer of the same texture belong to one soil type. Miami silt loam and the Miami loam are two soil types of the Blount Series, the differentiation within the series, therefore, being based on texture.

The detailed soil maps are valuable for the precise work dealing with conservation measures, land-capability studies, and the like, but it is the general soil that gives a person wanting an overall view of an area the most help. The *soil association* is a grouping of soils giving a greater degree of generalization than the soil-series maps. By grouping soils in this way, the complexity of the soil map is greatly reduced and the patterns of the soil groups become more obvious (often revealing a relationship to major physiographic features).

The relationship of two soil associations to the landforms (floodplains and terraces; rolling till uplands) of a part of Allen County are portrayed in Figure 38.2.

These diagrams are provided in the soil-survey reports to give a more detailed view of the topographic position of the soil associations. The associations portrayed in Figure 38.2 are the Eel-Martinsville-Genesee Association and the Morley-Blount Association.

Eel-Martinsville-Genesee Association.   This association consists of narrow bottom-lands and fairly wide stream terraces. Eel and Genesee soils are on the bottomlands, and Martinsville soils are on the stream terraces. Eel soils make up about 45% of the acreage, Martinsville soils about 45%, and Genesee soils about 10%. The association occupies about 4% of the county.

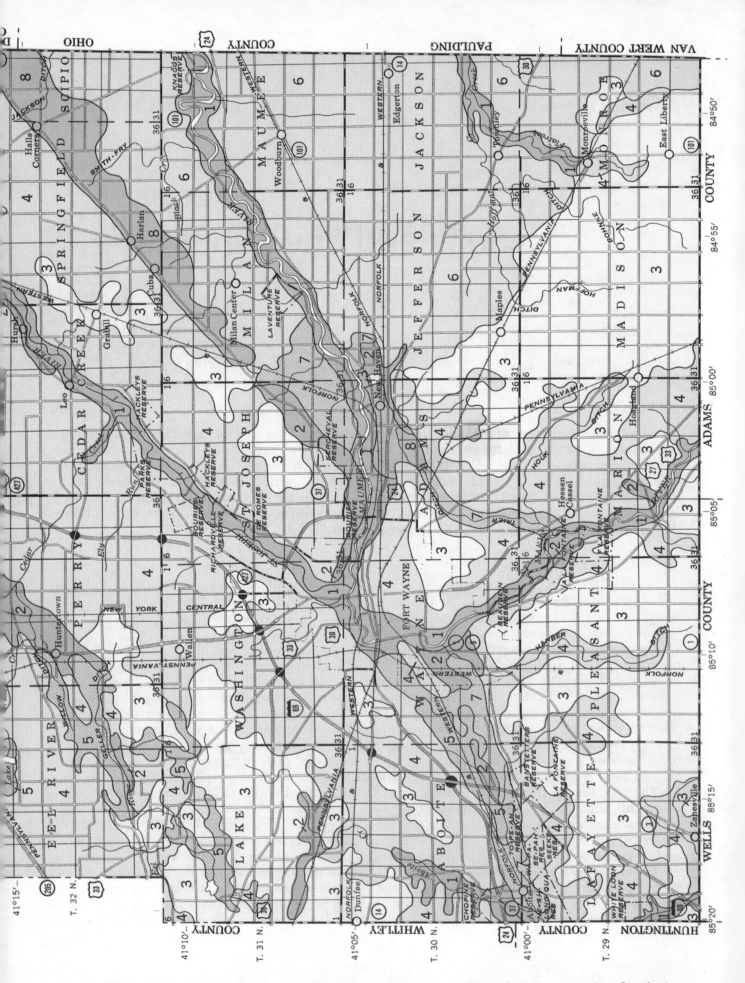

Figure 38.1.   General soil map, Allen County, Indiana (USDA, Soil Conservation Service)

General Soil Map, Allen County, Indiana
Soil Associations

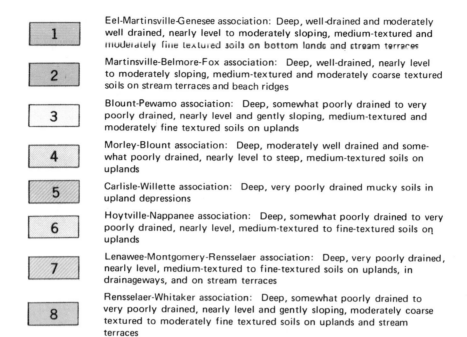

1 — Eel-Martinsville-Genesee association: Deep, well-drained and moderately well drained, nearly level to moderately sloping, medium-textured and moderately fine textured soils on bottom lands and stream terraces

2 — Martinsville-Belmore-Fox association: Deep, well-drained, nearly level to moderately sloping, medium-textured and moderately coarse textured soils on stream terraces and beach ridges

3 — Blount-Pewamo association: Deep, somewhat poorly drained to very poorly drained, nearly level and gently sloping, medium-textured and moderately fine textured soils on uplands

4 — Morley-Blount association: Deep, moderately well drained and somewhat poorly drained, nearly level to steep, medium-textured soils on uplands

5 — Carlisle-Willette association: Deep, very poorly drained mucky soils in upland depressions

6 — Hoytville-Nappanee association: Deep, somewhat poorly drained to very poorly drained, nearly level, medium-textured to fine-textured soils on uplands

7 — Lenawee-Montgomery-Rensselaer association: Deep, very poorly drained, nearly level, medium-textured to fine-textured soils on uplands, in drainageways, and on stream terraces

8 — Rensselaer-Whitaker association: Deep, somewhat poorly drained to very poorly drained, nearly level and gently sloping, moderately coarse textured to moderately fine textured soils on uplands and stream terraces

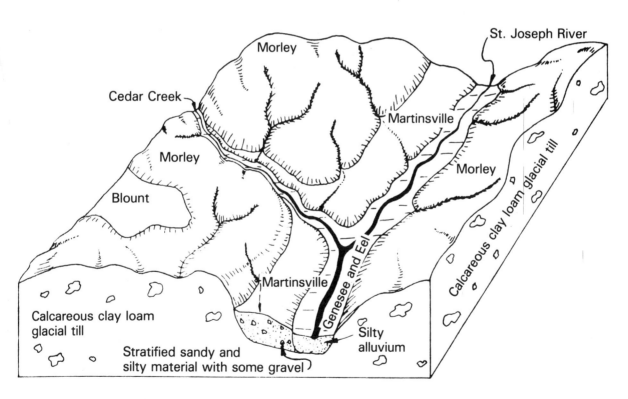

Figure 38.2. Topographic positions of the Eel-Martinsville-Genesee and the Morley-Blount associations (UDSA, 1969, *Allen County, Indiana, soil survey report*, pp. 2-5)

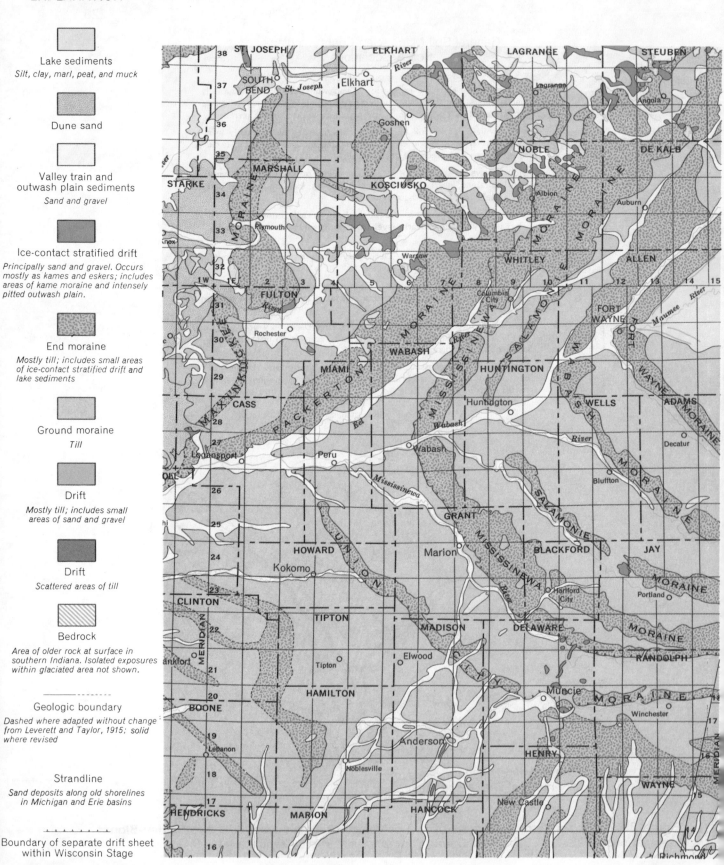

EXPLANATION

Lake sediments
Silt, clay, marl, peat, and muck

Dune sand

Valley train and outwash plain sediments
Sand and gravel

Ice-contact stratified drift

Principally sand and gravel. Occurs mostly as kames and eskers; includes areas of kame moraine and intensely pitted outwash plain.

End moraine

Mostly till; includes small areas of ice-contact stratified drift and lake sediments

Ground moraine
Till

Drift

Mostly till; includes small areas of sand and gravel

Drift

Scattered areas of till

Bedrock

Area of older rock at surface in southern Indiana. Isolated exposures within glaciated area not shown.

Geologic boundary

Dashed where adapted without change from Leverett and Taylor, 1915; solid where revised

Strandline

Sand deposits along old shorelines in Michigan and Erie basins

Boundary of separate drift sheet within Wisconsin Stage

Buried boundary of Kansan Stage drift
Inferred

Figure 38.3.   Glacial geology of Indiana (Indiana Geological Survey, *Atlas of mineral resources of Indiana,* map 10)

Eel soils are nearly level and are moderately well drained. They have a surface layer of dark grayish-brown loam or silt loam, underlain mostly by dark yellowish brown, mottled silty clay loam.

Martinsville soils are nearly level to moderately sloping and are well drained. They have a surface layer of grayish brown and dark grayish brown loam or silt loam and a subsoil that is mostly yellowish brown and reddish brown sandy clay loam.

Genesee soils are nearly level and are well drained. They have a surface layer of dark grayish brown loam to silty clay loam underlain by dark yellowish brown and yellowish brown loam.

The soils in this association are well suited to meadow and to corn, soybeans, and small grain. Occasional flooding on the Eel and Genesee soils may destroy or severely damage small grain. The Martinsville soils are subject to erosion.

Morley-Blount Association. This association is in upland areas, mostly in the northern two thirds of the county but not on the Lake Maumee Plain. Morley soils make up about 50% of the acreage, and Blount soils about 40%. Small areas of Pewamo soils and of other soils make up the remaining 10%. This association occupies about 40% of the county.

Morley soils are gently sloping to steep and are moderately well drained. They have a surface layer of grayish brown and very dark grayish brown silt loam and a subsoil that is mostly dark yellowish brown and brown clay and is mottled in the lower part.

Blount soils are nearly level and gently sloping and are somewhat poorly drained. They have a surface layer of dark grayish brown and very dark grayish brown mottled silty clay and clay.

The more gently sloping soils in this association are suited to meadow crops and to corn, soybeans, and small grain, but the strongly sloping and steep soils are kept as permanent pasture or maintained in native vegetation. Erosion is a hazard, and wetness is a limitation. (USDA, 1969, *Allen County, Indiana, soil survey report*, pp. 2–5)

PROBLEMS

In preparation for answering the questions that follow, compare and study the distribution of soil associations and glacial landforms in Figure 38.1 and Figure 38.3.

1. Explain the reason for the lobate nature of the moraines in northeastern Indiana.

2. Why are there river valleys running parallel to the morainal ridges? Examine the branch of the Wabash River that runs parallel to the Salamonie Moraine in Huntington and Wells counties.

3. List the soil associations associated with the following landforms:

   a. Terminal moraine _____

   b. Till plain (ground moraine) _____

   c. Sites of former lakes _____

   d. Floodplains _____

4. Besides the nature of the sedimentary deposits, what other evidence is there that a lake existed east of Fort Wayne?

5. a. Why are soils of the Hoytville-Nappanee Association poorly drained?

    b. If you were instructed to make a map of the floodplains of the largest streams on the map, what association would you use as a guide?
        _____

    c. On the geology map there are strandlines (old beach deposits). What kind of texture would you expect of soils found on these features?

    d. Which soil association is most closely associated with a particular geologic feature on these maps? (That is, what soil and geologic feature have the most similar pattern?)

6. What is the most frequently occurring soil problem in the area of the soil map?

7. What is the scale of the soil map (Figure 38.1)?

8. On a separate sheet of paper, draw a schematic cross section of the geology from Tipton (Tipton County) to Decatur (Adams County). Use Figure 38.3 for guidance.
9. Using the soil associations of Allen County as a guide, describe the probable soil conditions on the crest areas of the end moraine shown by the cross section in question 8.

EXERCISE **39**

Aerial Photographs: Additional Examples

In the previous exercises the aerial photographs selected for analysis have been assembled into stereo pairs, a technique that aids beginning interpreters. However, when one is working with aerial photographs as a field or laboratory tool, complete photographs are used, not stereo pairs.

The ideal way to use the photographs is with a mirror stereoscope (Figure 39.1). This instrument permits easier manipulation of the photographs and brings the entire area of overlap into stereoscopic vision.

Figure 39.1. Mirror stereoscope with photographs in position for viewing (Courtesy Wild Heerbrugg Instruments, Inc.)

Figure 39.2.   Isachsen Dome (Geological Survey of Canada A16192—20 and 21)

The bedrock of the area shown in Figure 39.2 has been folded into a distinctive dome. Erosion reveals the pattern of the sedimentary beds and an intricate drainage pattern.

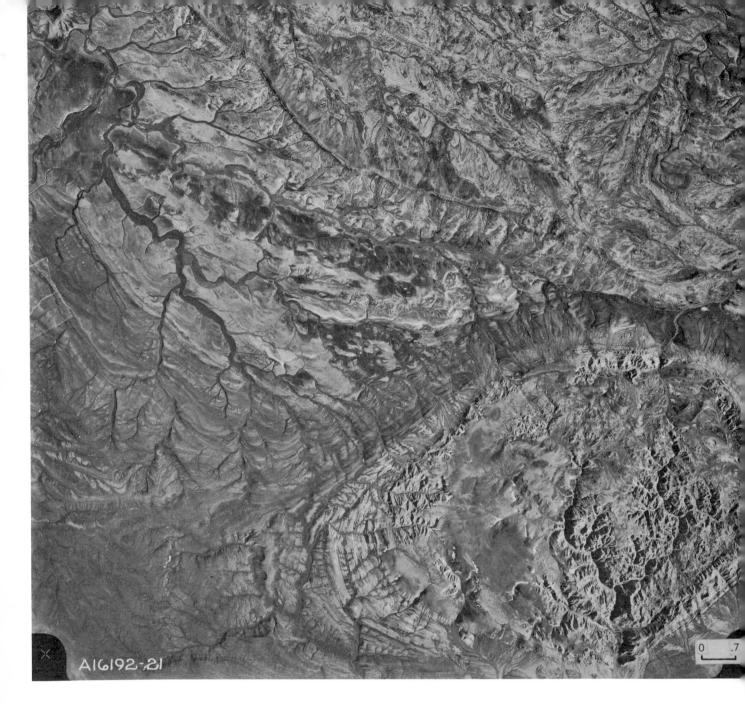

A16192-21

0 .7

PROBLEMS

1. Place six arrows around the dome (use a colored pencil); the arrows should point down the dip.
2. Compare the rocks on the outside of the dome with the ones in the center.
3. Draw a schematic (simplified) cross section across the dome.
4. Using your textbook, list three other examples of domes.

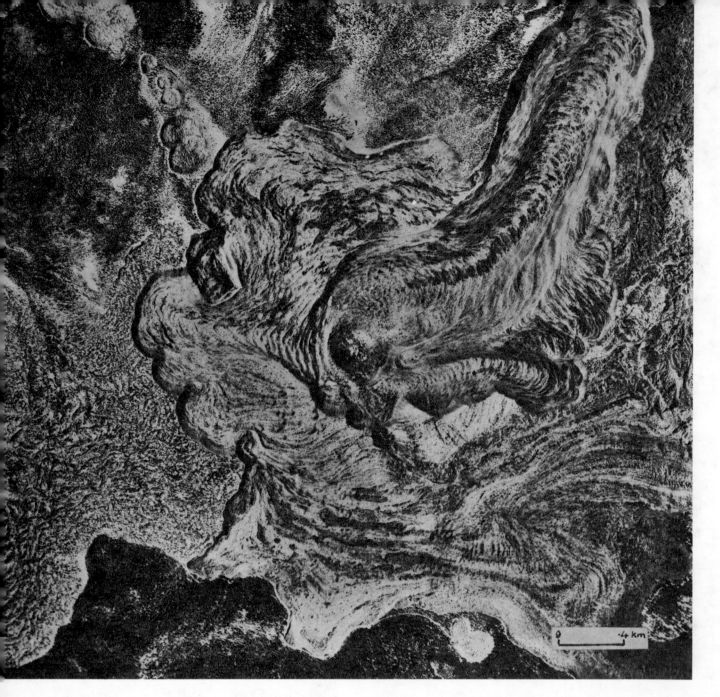

Figure 39.3.   Obsidian lava flows and domes (USGS Professional Paper 590)

The viscous nature of lava formed from obsidian is quite evident in the photographs in Figure 39.3. The steep front and edges of the flow are visible, as are the parallel ridges reflecting the flow of the lava.

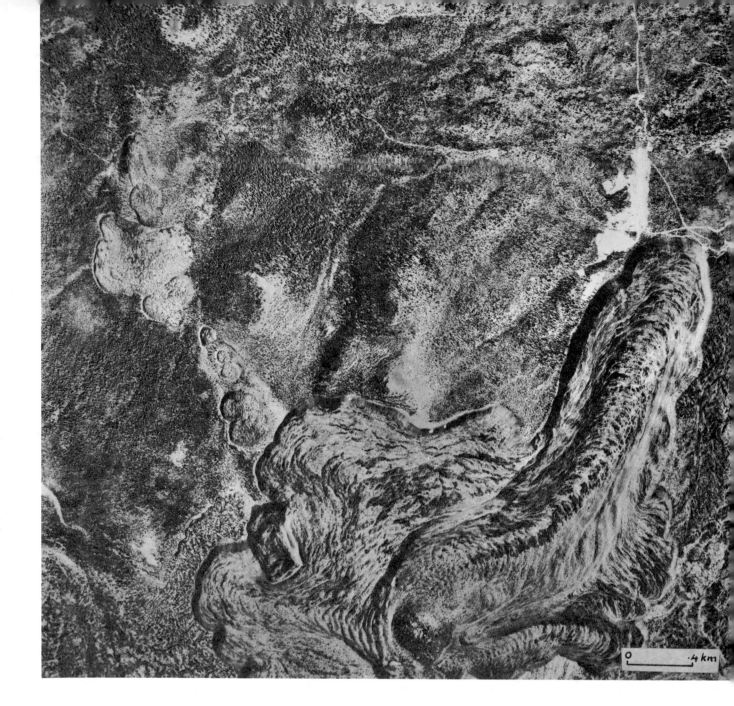

.4 km

PROBLEMS

5. Show the flow paths of the lava from the main vent by inserting arrows on the photographs.

6. Trending northwest to southeast there is a line of small cones.

a. Provide a possible explanation for the linear trend of the cones.

b. Are these cones younger or older than the steep-fronted lava flow found to the southeast?

7. Is there evidence on these photographs of earlier lava flows?

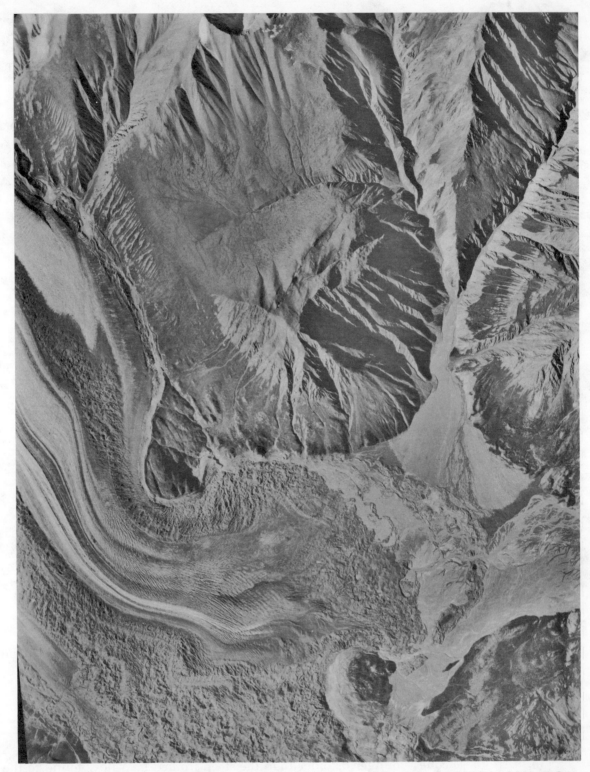

Figure 39.4.   Kaskawulsh Glacier (Geological Survey of Canada A15517—20 and 21)

A wide variety of spectacular features of glaciation are illustrated in Figure 39.4.

0   .7 km

PROBLEMS

8. Identify and label on the photographs the following features: lateral and medial moraines, cirque glaciers, icefalls, arêtes, truncated spurs, and a crevasse pattern.
9. Show with arrows the direction of flow of the main valley glaciers.

APPENDIX A
The Metric System

Units of measurement used in different parts of the world have varied from time immemorial. Repeated efforts through history have gradually led to greater and greater standardization. As communications improved over the centuries and people and goods moved about ever more freely, a pressing need for uniformity developed. The imperial system of measurement, that utilizing the foot, pound, degree Fahrenheit, and mile, was widely disseminated by the British during the heyday of their empire.

In 1790, the French (bless their hearts) introduced the metric system, a system based upon decimalization. Initially, the spread of the metric system was aided by its adoption by a Europe dominated by Napoleonic France and by its use in the French colonies. The metric system has gained greater and greater favor among nations of the world so that by 1972 the only major industrialized nation not either fully using the metric system or in the process of adopting it was the United States. Several small countries not using the metric system are Ceylon, Gambia, Guyana, Jamaica, Liberia, Malawi, and Sierra Leone.

The advantages of the metric system are many, including the universality and the basic decimal character of the system. The system that is now being favored around the world is the "System International" or SI which was adopted by an international committee in 1960 and has since been adopted as official by more than 30 countries. The advantages of the metric system have led some sectors of the American economy to adopt the metric system long ago. The chemical industry is an example. If the United States is to play a major role in world affairs, it must adopt the system of measure used by the rest of the world. Most American scientific journals now require that the metric system of measurement be used either alone or in conjunction with the imperial system. The National Aeronautics and Space Administration (NASA) in November 1970 became the first official U.S. government agency to convert to the metric system. A bill was introduced in Congress in 1972 to have the SI adopted as the official system for the United States, but the bill did not pass. There can be no doubt that it will eventually be approved.

The basic units in the metric system are either divided into a thousand parts or, to make larger units, multiples of one thousand are used.

Table A.1. Metric Prefixes and Symbols

	Basic Unit	Arabic Notation	Prefix	Symbol
Multiples	10^6	1,000,000	mega	M
	10^3	1000	kilo	k
	10^2	100	hecto	h
	10	10	deka	da
Fractions	10^{-1}	0.1	deci	d
	10^{-2}	0.01	centi	c
	10^{-3}	0.001	milli	m
	10^{-6}	0.000001	micro	μ

Note: Although fractions and multiples of 10 and 100 are shown in the table, the use of these units is discouraged. Multiples of 1000 are preferred.

Table A.2. Imperial Variables to Metric Variables

Physical Variable	Unit	SI Equivalent
Length	Inch	25.44 mm
	Foot	0.305 m
	Yard	0.914 m
	Mile	1.61 km
Area	Square inch	645.2 mm²
	Square foot	0.093 m²
	Square yard	0.836 m²
	Acre	4047 m²
	Square mile	2.59 km²
Velocity	Foot/second	0.305 m/s^{-1}
	Mile/hour	0.447 m/s^{-1}
Mass	Pound	0.454 kg
Density	Pounds/cubic foot	16.02 kg/m^{-3}
Pressure	Standard atmosphere	101.3 kN/m^{-2}
	Pound/square inch	6895 N/m^{-2}
Temperature	Fahrenheit	$°F = (9/5) \,°C + 32$

Table A.3. Conversion of Standard Metric Units to Imperial Units

	Standard Metric Unit	Imperial Equivalent
Length	Kilometer (km)	0.621 mile
	Meter (m)	1.094 yards
		39.370 inches
		3.281 feet
Area	Hectare (ha)	
	Square kilometer (km²)	2.471 acres
	Square meter (m²)	1.196 square yards
Volume	Cubic meter (m³)	1.308 cubic yards
	Liter (l)	0.264 gallons
Velocity	Kilometers per hour (km/h)	0.621 miles per hour
	Meters per second (m/s)	3.281 feet per second
Mass	Kilogram (kg)	2.205 pounds
	Gram (g)	0.035 ounce

Table A.4. Proportional Parts for Degrees Celsius and Fahrenheit

°C	°F	°C	°F
.56	1	1	1.8
1.11	2	2	3.6
1.67	3	3	5.4
2.22	4	4	7.2
2.78	5	5	9.0
3.33	6	6	10.8
3.89	7	7	12.6
4.44	8	8	14.4
5.00	9	9	16.2

Key to Weather Maps

TEMPERATURE MAP

Temperature data are entered from selected weather stations in the United States. The figures entered above the station dot denote maximum temperatures reported from these stations during the 24 hours ending 1:00 a.m., E.S.T.; the figures entered below the station dot denote minimum temperature during the 24 hours ending at 1:00 p.m., E.S.T., of the previous day. The letter "M" denotes missing data. Shaded areas labeled "HIGHER" or "LOWER" indicate the areas where temperatures recorded at 1:00 a.m., E.S.T., are at least 10° warmer or colder than 24 hours ago.

PRECIPITATION MAP

Precipitation data are entered from selected weather stations in the United States. When precipitation has occurred at any of these stations in the 24-hour period ending at 1:00 a.m., E.S.T., the total amount, in inches and hundredths, is entered above the station dot. When the figures for total precipitation have been compiled from incomplete data and entered on the map, the amount is underlined. "T" indicates a trace of precipitation, and the letter "M" denotes missing data. The geographical areas where precipitation has fallen during the 24 hours ending at 1:00 a.m., E.S.T., are shaded.

CONTINENTAL MAP

The insert map of nearly the entire North American continent shows the surface pressure pattern and frontal analysis twelve hours earlier than the principal map. Areas of precipitation at map time are shaded.

SURFACE FORECAST MAP

The insert map portrays surface pressure and frontal patterns expected at 7:00 p.m., E.S.T. today, or 18 hours after the principal map. Comparison of this map with the principal map will show forecast movements and changes in the surface pressure and frontal patterns.

500-MILLIBAR MAP

Contour lines, isotherms, and wind arrows are shown on the insert map for the 500-millibar contour level. Solid lines are drawn to show height above sea level and are labeled in feet. Dashed lines are drawn at 5 intervals of temperature, and labeled in degrees Celsius. A temperature conversion table is shown in block **13**. True wind direction is shown by "arrows" which are plotted as flying with the wind. The wind speed is shown by flags and feathers, each flag representing 50 knots, each full feather 10 knots, and each half-feather 5 knots. For conversion to miles per hour, refer to block **9**.

INQUIRIES

Inquiries regarding these maps may be addressed to Chief, U. S. Weather Bureau, Washington, D. C., 20235.

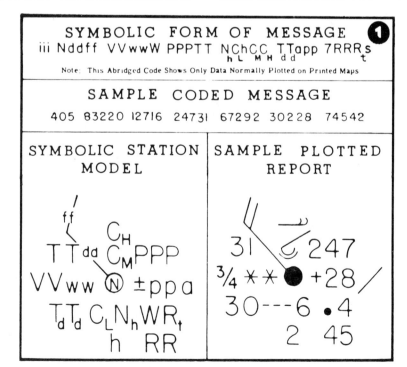

EXPLANATION OF SYMBOLS AND MAP ENTRIES

Symbols in order as they appear in the message	Explanation of symbols and decode of example above	Remarks on coding and plotting
iii	Station number 405 = Washington	Usually printed on manuscript maps below station circle. Omitted on Daily Weather Map in favor of printed station names.
N	Total amount of cloud 8 = completely covered	Observed in tenths of cloud cover and coded in Oktas (eighths) according to code table in Block [6]. Plotted in symbols shown in same table.
dd	True direction from which wind is blowing 32 = 320° = NW	Coded in tens of degrees and plotted as the shaft of an arrow extending from the station circle toward the direction from which the wind is blowing.
ff	Wind speed in knots 20 = 20 knots	Coded in knots (nautical miles per hour) and plotted as feathers and half-feathers representing 10 and 5 knots, respectively, on the shaft of the wind direction arrow. See block [6].
VV	Visibility in miles and fractions 12 = 12/16 or 3/4 miles	Decoded and plotted in miles and fractions up to 3 1/8 miles. Visibilities above 3 1/8 miles but less than 10 miles are plotted to the nearest whole mile. Values higher than 10 miles are omitted from the map.
ww	Present weather 71 = continuous slight snow	Coded in figures taken from the "ww" table (block [9]) and plotted in the corresponding symbols same block. Entries for code figures 00, 01, 02, and 03 are omitted from this map.
W	Past weather 6 = rain	Coded in figures taken from the "W" table (block [11]) and plotted in the corresponding symbols same block. No entry made for code figures 0, 1, or 2.
ppp	Barometric Pressure (in millibars) reduced to sea-level 247 = 1024.7 mb.	Coded and plotted in tens, units, and tenths of millibars. The initial 9 or 10 and the decimal point are omitted. See block [12].
TT	Current air temperature 31 = 31° F.	Coded and plotted in actual value in whole degrees F. See block [13].
N_h	Fraction of sky covered by low or middle cloud 6 = 7 or 8 tenths	Observed and coded in tenths of cloud cover. Plotted on map as code figure in message. See block [7].

[2]

Symbol	Explanation	Remarks
C_L	Cloud type 7 = Fractostratus and/or Fractocumulus of bad weather (scud)	Predominating clouds of types in C_L table (block [3]) are coded from that table and plotted in corresponding symbols.
h	Height of base of cloud 2 = 300 to 599 feet	Observed in feet and coded and plotted as code figures according to code table in block [5].
C_M	Cloud type 9 = Altocumulus of chaotic sky	See C_M table in block [3].
C_H	Cloud type 2 = Dense cirrus in patches	See C_H table in block [3].
$T_d T_d$	Temperature of dewpoint 30 = 30° F.	Coded and plotted in actual value in whole degrees F.
a	Characteristic of barograph trace 2 = rising steadily or unsteadily	Coded according to table in block [10] and plotted in corresponding symbols.
pp	Pressure change in 3 hours preceding observation 28 - 2.8 millibars	Coded and plotted in units and tenths of millibars.
7	Indicator figure	Not plotted.
RR	Amount of precipitation 45 = 0.45 inches	Coded and plotted in inches to the nearest hundredth of an inch.
R_t	Time precipitation began or ended 4 = 3 to 4 hours ago	Coded and plotted in figures from table in block [4].
s	Depth of snow on ground	Not plotted.

CLOUD ABBREVIATION / C_L

C_L	CLOUD ABBREVIATION	DESCRIPTION (Abridged From W.M.O. Code)
1	St or Fs - Stratus or Fractostratus	Cu of fair weather, little vertical development and seemingly flattened
2	Ci - Cirrus	Cu of considerable development, generally towering, with or without other Cu or Sc bases all at same level
3	Cs - Cirrostratus	Cb with tops lacking clear-cut outlines, but distinctly not cirriform or anvil-shaped; with or without Cu, Sc, or St
4	Cc - Cirrocumulus	Sc formed by spreading out of Cu; Cu often present also
5	Ac - Altocumulus	Sc not formed by spreading out of Cu
6	As - Altostratus	St or Fs or both, but no Fs of bad weather
7	Sc - Stratocumulus	Fs and/or Fc of bad weather (scud)
8	Ns - Nimbostratus	Cu and Sc (not formed by spreading out of Cu) with bases at different levels
9	Cu or Fc - Cumulus or Fractocumulus	Cb having a clearly fibrous (cirriform) top, often anvil-shaped, with or without Cu, Sc, St, or scud
	Cb - Cumulonimbus	

③ C_M DESCRIPTION (Abridged From W.M.O. Code)

C_M	DESCRIPTION
1	Thin As (most of cloud layer semi-transparent)
2	Thick As, greater part sufficiently dense to hide sun (or moon), or Ns
3	Thin Ac, mostly semi-transparent; cloud elements not changing much and at a single level
4	Thin Ac in patches; cloud elements continually changing and/or occurring at more than one level
5	Thin Ac in bands or in a layer gradually spreading over sky and usually thickening as a whole
6	Ac formed by the spreading out of Cu
7	Double-layered Ac, or a thick layer of Ac, not increasing, or Ac with As and/or Ns
8	Ac in the form of Cu-shaped tufts or Ac with turrets
9	Ac of a chaotic sky, usually at different levels; patches of dense Ci are usually present also

③ C_H DESCRIPTION (Abridged From W.M.O. Code)

C_H	DESCRIPTION
1	Filaments of Ci, or "mares tails," scattered and not increasing
2	Dense Ci in patches or twisted sheaves, usually not increasing, sometimes like remains of Cb, or towers or tufts
3	Dense Ci, often anvil-shaped, derived from or associated with Cb
4	Ci, often hook-shaped, gradually spreading over the sky and usually thickening as a whole
5	Ci and Cs, often in converging bands, or Cs alone; generally overspreading and growing denser; the continuous layer not reaching 45° altitude
6	Ci and Cs, often in converging bands, or Cs alone; generally overspreading and growing denser; the continuous layer exceeding 45° altitude
7	Veil of Cs covering the entire sky
8	Cs not increasing and not covering entire sky
9	Cc alone or Cc with some Ci or Cs, but the Cc being the main cirriform cloud

④ R_t TIME OF PRECIPITATION

R_t	TIME OF PRECIPITATION
0	No Precipitation
1	Less than 1 hour ago
2	1 to 2 hours ago
3	2 to 3 hours ago
4	3 to 4 hours ago
5	4 to 5 hours ago
6	5 to 6 hours ago
7	6 to 12 hours ago
8	More than 12 hours ago
9	Unknown

⑤ h HEIGHT

h	HEIGHT IN FEET (Rounded Off)	HEIGHT IN METERS (Approximate)
0	0 - 149	0 - 49
1	150 - 299	50 - 99
2	300 - 599	100 - 199
3	600 - 999	200 - 299
4	1,000 - 1,999	300 - 599
5	2,000 - 3,499	600 - 999
6	3,500 - 4,999	1,000 - 1,499
7	5,000 - 6,499	1,500 - 1,999
8	6,500 - 7,999	2,000 - 2,499
9	At or above 8,000, or no clouds	At or above 2,500, or no clouds

⑥ N SKY COVERAGE (Total Amount)

N	SKY COVERAGE
0	No clouds
1	Less than one-tenth or one-tenth
2	Two-tenths or three-tenths
3	Four-tenths
4	Five-tenths
5	Six-tenths
6	Seven-tenths or eight-tenths
7	Nine-tenths or overcast with openings
8	Completely overcast
9	Sky obscured

⑦ N_h SKY COVERAGE (Low And/Or Middle Clouds)

N_h	SKY COVERAGE
0	No clouds
1	Less than one-tenth or one-tenth
2	Two-tenths or three-tenths
3	Four-tenths
4	Five-tenths
5	Six-tenths
6	Seven-tenths or eight-tenths
7	Nine-tenths or overcast with openings
8	Completely overcast
9	Sky obscured

WW PRESENT WEATHER (Descriptions Abridged from W. M. O. Code) ⑧

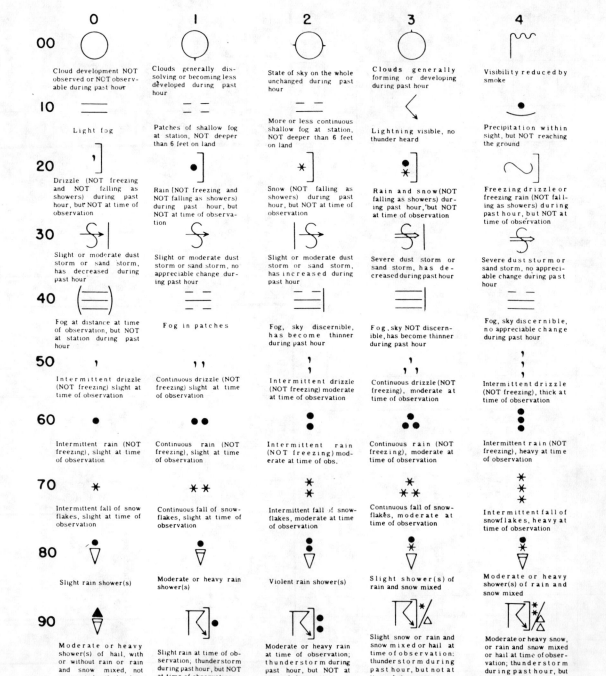

0

00 — Cloud development NOT observed or NOT observable during past hour

10 — Light fog

20 — Drizzle (NOT freezing and NOT falling as showers) during past hour, but NOT at time of observation

30 — Slight or moderate dust storm or sand storm, has decreased during past hour

40 — Fog at distance at time of observation, but NOT at station during past hour

50 — Intermittent drizzle (NOT freezing) slight at time of observation

60 — Intermittent rain (NOT freezing), slight at time of observation

70 — Intermittent fall of snow flakes, slight at time of observation

80 — Slight rain shower(s)

90 — Moderate or heavy shower(s) of hail, with or without rain or rain and snow mixed, not associated with thunder

1

Clouds generally dissolving or becoming less developed during past hour

Patches of shallow fog at station, NOT deeper than 6 feet on land

Rain (NOT freezing and NOT falling as showers) during past hour, but NOT at time of observation

Slight or moderate dust storm or sand storm, no appreciable change during past hour

Fog in patches

Continuous drizzle (NOT freezing) slight at time of observation

Continuous rain (NOT freezing), slight at time of observation

Continuous fall of snowflakes, slight at time of observation

Moderate or heavy rain shower(s)

Slight rain at time of observation, thunderstorm during past hour, but NOT at time of observation

2

State of sky on the whole unchanged during past hour

More or less continuous shallow fog at station, NOT deeper than 6 feet on land

Snow (NOT falling as showers) during past hour, but NOT at time of observation

Slight or moderate dust storm or sand storm, has increased during past hour

Fog, sky discernible, has become thinner during past hour

Intermittent drizzle (NOT freezing) moderate at time of observation

Intermittent rain (NOT freezing) moderate at time of obs.

Intermittent fall of snowflakes, moderate at time of observation

Violent rain shower(s)

Moderate or heavy rain at time of observation; thunderstorm during past hour, but NOT at time of observation

3

Clouds generally forming or developing during past hour

Lightning visible, no thunder heard

Rain and snow (NOT falling as showers) during past hour, but NOT at time of observation

Severe dust storm or sand storm, has decreased during past hour

Fog, sky NOT discernible, has become thinner during past hour

Continuous drizzle (NOT freezing), moderate at time of observation

Continuous rain (NOT freezing), moderate at time of observation

Continuous fall of snowflakes, moderate at time of observation

Slight shower(s) of rain and snow mixed

Slight snow or rain and snow mixed or hail at time of observation; thunderstorm during past hour, but not at time of observation

4

Visibility reduced by smoke

Precipitation within sight, but NOT reaching the ground

Freezing drizzle or freezing rain (NOT falling as showers) during past hour, but NOT at time of observation

Severe dust storm or sand storm, no appreciable change during past hour

Fog, sky discernible, no appreciable change during past hour

Intermittent drizzle (NOT freezing), thick at time of observation

Intermittent rain (NOT freezing), heavy at time of observation

Intermittent fall of snowflakes, heavy at time of observation

Moderate or heavy shower(s) of rain and snow mixed

Moderate or heavy snow, or rain and snow mixed or hail at time of observation; thunderstorm during past hour, but NOT at time of obs.

WW PRESENT WEATHER (Descriptions Abridged from W. M. O. Code)

	5	6	7	8	9
00	Haze	Widespread dust in suspension in the air, NOT raised by wind, at time of observation	Dust or sand raised by wind, at time of observation	Well developed dust devil(s) within past hour	Dust storm or sand storm within sight of or at station during past hour
10	Precipitation within sight, reaching the ground, but distant from station	Precipitation within sight, reaching the ground, near to but NOT at station	Thunder heard, but no precipitation at the station	Squall(s) within sight during past hour	Funnel cloud(s) within sight during past hour
20	Showers of rain during past hour, but NOT at time of observation	Showers of snow, or of rain and snow, during past hour, but NOT at time of observation	Showers of hail, or of hail and rain, during past hour, but NOT at time of observation	Fog during past hour, but NOT at time of observation	Thunderstorm (with or without precipitation) during past hour, but NOT at time of obs.
30	Severe dust storm or sand storm, has increased during past hour	Slight or moderate drifting snow, generally low	Heavy drifting snow, generally low	Slight or moderate drifting snow, generally high	Heavy drifting snow, generally high
40	Fog, sky NOT discernible, no appreciable change during past hour	Fog, sky discernible, has begun or become thicker during past hour	Fog, sky NOT discernible, has begun or become thicker during past hour	Fog, depositing rime, sky discernible	Fog, depositing rime, sky NOT discernible
50	Continuous drizzle (NOT freezing), thick at time of observation	Slight freezing drizzle	Moderate or thick freezing drizzle	Drizzle and rain, slight	Drizzle and rain, moderate or heavy
60	Continuous rain (NOT freezing), heavy at time of observation	Slight freezing rain	Moderate or heavy freezing rain	Rain or drizzle and snow, slight	Rain or drizzle and snow, moderate or heavy
70	Continuous fall of snowflakes, heavy at time of observation	Ice needles (with or without fog)	Granular snow (with or without fog)	Isolated starlike snow crystals (with or without fog)	Ice pellets (sleet, U. S. definition)
80	Slight snow shower(s)	Moderate or heavy snow shower(s)	Slight shower(s) of soft or small hail with or without rain, or rain and snow mixed	Moderate or heavy shower(s) of soft or small hail with or without rain, or rain and snow mixed	Slight shower(s) of hail, with or without rain or rain and snow mixed, not associated with thunder
90	Slight or moderate thunderstorm without hail, but with rain and/or snow at time of obs.	Slight or moderate thunderstorm, with hail at time of observation	Heavy thunderstorm, without hail, but with rain and/or snow at time of observation	Thunderstorm combined with dust storm or sand storm at time of obs.	Heavy thunderstorm with hail at time of observation

ff	(MILES) (Statute) Per Hour	**9** KNOTS	Code Number	a	**10** BAROMETRIC TENDENCY	
◎	Calm	Calm	0	⌒	Rising, then falling	
—	1 - 2	1 - 2	1	⟋	Rising, then steady; or rising, then rising more slowly	Barometer now higher than 3 hours ago
⎯⌐	3 - 8	3 - 7	2	⟋	Rising steadily, or unsteadily	
⎯⟍	9 - 14	8 - 12	3	✓	Falling or steady, then rising; or rising, then rising more quickly	
⎯⟍	15 - 20	13 - 17	4	—	Steady, same as 3 hours ago	
⎯⟍⟍	21 - 25	18 - 22	5	⟍	Falling, then rising, same or lower than 3 hours ago	Barometer now lower than 3 hours ago
⎯⟍⟍⟍	26 - 31	23 - 27	6	⟍	Falling, then steady; or falling, then falling more slowly	
⎯⟍⟍⟍	32 - 37	28 - 32	7	⟍	Falling steadily, or unsteadily	
⎯⟍⟍⟍⟍	38 - 43	33 - 37	8	⌒	Steady or rising, then falling; or falling, then falling more quickly	

			Code Number	W	**11** PAST WEATHER	
⎯⟍⟍⟍⟍	44 - 49	38 - 42	0		Clear or few clouds	Not Plotted
⎯⟍⟍⟍⟍⟍	50 - 54	43 - 47	1		Partly cloudy (scattered) or variable sky	
⎯◣	55 - 60	48 - 52	2		Cloudy (broken) or overcast	
⎯◣	61 - 66	53 - 57	3	↭ / ⇥	Sandstorm or dust-storm, or drifting or blowing snow	
⎯◣⟍	67 - 71	58 - 62	4	≡	Fog, or smoke, or thick dust haze	
⎯◣⟍	72 - 77	63 - 67	5	،	Drizzle	
⎯◣⟍⟍	78 - 83	68 - 72	6	●	Rain	
⎯◣⟍⟍	84 - 89	73 - 77	7	✳	Snow, or rain and snow mixed, or ice pellets (sleet)	
⎯◣◣	119 - 123	103 - 107	8	▽	Shower(s)	
			9	⟅	Thunderstorm, with or without precipitation	

APPENDIX C
Soil Classification

Table C.1. A List of Diagnostic Horizons
Used for the Differentiation of Orders in U.S. Soil Classification

Epipedons	
Mollic epipedon	Histic epipedon
Anthropic epipedon	Plaggen epipedon
Umbric epipedon	Ochric epipedon

Subsurface Horizons	
Argillic horizon	Fragipan
Agric horizon	Albic horizon
Natric horizon	Calcic and ca horizon
Sombric horizon	Gypsic horizon
Spodic horizon	Petrocalcic horizon
Placic horizon	Petrogypsic horizon
Cambic horizon	Salic horizon
Oxic horizon	Sulfuric horizon
Duripan	

Source: USDA, 1975, Agricultural Handbook No. 436.

Table C.2. U.S. Soil Classification (orders)

Alfisol	Soils with clay accumulation in subsurface horizons.
Aridisol	Soils of arid climates (desert soils).
Entisol	Soils lacking diagnostic horizons.
Histosol	Organic soils usually formed from peat in places with high water tables.
Inceptisol	Weakly developed or absent soil horizons; has at least 3 mo of soil moisture for plant growth; little accumulation of translocated materials.
Mollisol	Soils with dark, organic-rich surface horizons; significant amounts of calcium; a soil typically associated with grasslands.
Oxisol	Soils with significant weathering of all minerals of the quartz; occur in tropical or subtropical areas.
Spodosol	The B horizon has an accumulation of black-red amorphous materials, above which is a light-colored (albic) horizon. Associated with forests in cool, moist climates.
Ultisol	Heavily leached soils with horizons of clay accumulation.
Vertisol	Soils with clays that swell when wet and develop cracks during dry seasons.

Source: USDA, 1975, Agricultural Handbook No. 436.

Table C.3. Soil Classification of Canada (orders)

Chernozemic	Dark-colored A horizons with high organic content; accumulation of lime carbonate in a lower part of the soil.
Solonetzic	Mineral soils with salinization (presence of alkaline salts); often with a clayey B horizon.
Luvisolic	Leached soils produced in a forest environment; concentration of clays in the B horizon; light-colored Ae horizon.
Podsolic	Distinguished by the accumulation of soluble organic matters and mobile compounds of aluminum of iron in the B horizon. Often have light-colored Ae horizon.
Brunisolic	A broad category of soils with a brown-colored Bm horizon differentiated by color, structure and composition from the A and C horizons.
Regosolic	A weakly developed soil profile though often with an organic surface layer. These soils reflect the parent materials from which they are formed.
Gleysolic	Poorly drained soils; reducing conditions leading to gleyed horizons with greenish-bluish colors.
Organic	Soil derived from organic deposits (e.g., peats).

Source: Agriculture Canada, 1977, Soils of Canada, Vol. 1. This report and the U.S. Department of Agriculture Agricultural Handbook No. 436 contain tables correlating the U.S. and Canadian soil classification systems.